# A Guide to the Ghosts of Lincoln

Printing history:
First edition, 1983. Three printings through 1984.
Second edition, 1987. Two prinitngs through 1990.


For Curt W. Kimball (1948-1978)
and for Sam Wilson


Copyright 1983, 1987 by Alan Boye


SALTILLO PRESS
57 Lafayette               ISBN 0-913473-08-1
St. Johnsbury, Vermont
05819

# A Guide to the Ghosts of Lincoln

## Second Edition

### by Alan Boye

SALTILLO PRESS

# Contents

Preface to the Second Edition......................*i*

Introduction...........................................*iii*

The C. C. White Building Ghost..................1

The Sailor..............................................9

A Woman in the Field—The Spirit at
        Antelope Park..............................15

A Cold Sidewalk and a Typical Lincoln Home:
        Two Hauntings off Washington Street.....20

Willa Cather and a Ghost Dog....................25

The Penitentiary Field............................31

A Walking Shadow's Hour Upon the Stage....37

A Potpourri..........................................42
        I. The Warehouse   II. A Place for the Willies   III. The Big House   IV. Grandpa

Shapes in the Fog Around Lake Street Lake...59

Robbers' Cave............................................64

The Pawnee Dance....................................70

Near Twenty-second and Harrison..............78

Bloody Mary's House...............................84

The Dorm..............................................97

The State Capitol Building......................105

Famous Paintings...................................111

The Strange Disappearance of
      Charles E. Danca......................121

Just Go East on "O"...............................131

# Preface to the Second Edition

Since the publication of the first edition of *A Guide to the Ghosts of Lincoln* in 1984 approximately 100 additional people have submitted stories about haunted places in eastern Nebraska. The best of these stories have been included in this second edition of the book.

In addition, many of the original stories have been updated to include recent events at those locations, so that this edition represents a new look at many of the area's famous haunted places.

As in the first edition, the stories represent the stories as told to the author. The names of people have been changed, as have the locations of private dwellings. However, the *general* locations given are the true locations of the actual occurrences.

It is said that an area does not really become alive until it has generated stories and tales. Likewise, it is said that one does not really belong to a place until one knows the folk tales and legends of the area. Toward those ends this book was written.

# Introduction

Ghosts are not new. For hundreds, perhaps thousands of years there have been reports of human and animal shapes passing through the air, through walls and vanishing like wisps of smoke.

Perhaps the strange, etched figures carved into the rocks and caves of ancient civilizations depicted apparitions alongside the stories of great hunts and other important events. In the 1700s several famous hauntings were recorded in diaries and letters. By the 1800s many "haunted houses" had become quite well known and their stories had even started to appear in the popular literature of the age.

In our own century such events have been met with a great deal of skepticism. This is logical, for in the age of Science as Master events which seem to ridicule the rules of physics are often met with cynicism. It seems absurd that ghosts could exist alongside of quantum physics, quasars and black holes.

It appears all the more implausible when these ghosts are reported in your own town, perhaps even in your own neighborhood, but for anyone who has stepped into a house, or walked along a country road and for a fleeting moment felt "something strange," the possibili-

## A Guide to the Ghosts of Lincoln

ty of a spirit world is not so remote.

Ghosts exist. Even if there aren't spirits who walk about, the events recorded in this book did *happen* to people. You may talk with any of them and you will soon realize that—even if they only imagined what they saw—the apparitions reported here are no less real to those who witnessed them. *Something* happened.

Even the greatest doubters will have to pause when they hear the story of hauntings that have been viewed by groups of individuals.

No two hauntings are alike, although there are similarities between every event that has been recorded during the last three hundred years.

Many hauntings are first noticed when objects in a house disappear, and then suddenly reappear weeks later. Several hauntings include reports of objects moving by themselves. Cupboard doors fly open and plates fall from their secure place on the shelf.

Often lights turn themselves off and on. Doorknobs turn. Water in a sink is turned on.

Although ghosts may not be visible to all, the noises that accompany apparitions are heard by everyone at the location.

One must be cautious when reporting noise as a phenomenon produced by a phantom, for oftentimes there is a physical explanation for the noise. Scraping in the wall might turn out to be a family of mice that have moved in for the winter. The banging on the floor might be nothing more than the hot water pipes expand-

# A Guide to the Ghosts of Lincoln

ing. However, when repeated noises are reported and no explanation is found, one should be suspicious.

Oftentimes the noise reported with a sighting is that of music, often a piano, or an organ. The music is soft, distant, like that in a dream. Many times people have reported hearing a voice, or a number of voices—their conversation muted and just beyond being comprehensible. Other times a distant solitary voice is heard, as in the case of the ghost at Antelope Park.

All of these manifestations seem to indicate that a spirit is trying to make itself known and that it wants to be recognized. However, there has yet to be a recorded case where a spirit has actually carried on a dialogue with a person. In fact, it is quite rare that a ghost will even acknowledge the existence of the living beings around it.

In all cases, even when a spirit has not been seen, a distinct atmosphere fills the air. Long before the famous ghost of the C.C. White Building was sighted, the students who used the building never failed to report that they "felt something strange" in the building. This sixth sense is a quality that accompanies every haunted location.

Although many of the above signs are present, it is a rare event when a phantom is actually sighted. As few as one in ten hauntings include the visible manifestation we have come to call ghosts. However, when one does appear, it leaves an indelible impression on the people who have seen it.

Not everyone can see a ghost. In may cases only one

## A Guide to the Ghosts of Lincoln

person in a group will report seeing something. This person might see the apparition a number of times, while the others see nothing. Other times the event will be visible to an entire group of people.

Many sightings are associated with a variety of distinct and powerful odors. These have been variously reported as "musty," "sulfurous," "sweet," "old," and so on. The existence of these odors is apparently one of the more powerful signs. The smells are almost always follwed by a visible manifestation.

There are a variety of explanations offered for the existence of ghosts. Perhaps the most popular explanation—at least in terms of movies and television shows—is that ghosts are the spirits of people who came to a violent or untimely end. This theory often matches historical information about a location, but does not take into account the occurrence of apparitions at locations where no historic evidence of a death can be found. A version of this theory is that a ghost will attach itself to a location, although the violent death happened elsewhere.

Another explanation for the existence of ghosts is that the viewer is witnessing a kind of film-loop—a recording of some event that happened in the past and endlessly repeats itself like a broken record. This idea contends that the house, or building, or field, has a kind of psychic film that records all events. Most events are so insignificant that they soon fade. However, once in a great while an event will occur that makes such a powerful image

## A Guide to the Ghosts of Lincoln

on the "psychic film" that it takes a long while for the image to fade. These events eventually become visible to a viewer who has an active and well-tuned psychic ability. This explains why certain apparitions are always viewed in the same location, and oftentimes are seen in the same pose. It could also account for the common sensation of so many people who "feel something strange" at a particular location.

This explanation makes the distinction that it is the *memory* of someone that haunts a location, not the actual spirit of the person.

Yet another theory, and one that skeptics and nonbelievers can appreciate, is that the hauntings are simply the creation of a person's over-active imagination. This is not to imply that the person has intentionally lied, but that an over-active imagination has created the manifestations.

This theory is easy to comprehend, especially for anyone who has slept outside with a friend when they were young. Chances were that before the night was over, you had created a variety of creatures from the sounds and the sights of the night. Those creatures were as real as the cold sleeping bag you tried to bury yourself into.

But, can the human imagination account for an actual *sighting*, especially one that is visible to a group of people? Perhaps the human mind, especially if involved with a group of people, is able to create images that are visible to all members of the group. It may be

# A Guide to the Ghosts of Lincoln

that houses are haunted by the group consciousness of the living, rather than the dead. Psychologist Carl Jung suggested just such a phenomenon for the explanation of the many sightings of U.F.O.s. Jung claimed that the human race, wanting proof of the existence of another world to give us hope for the future, desires to see such apparitions and, in effect, creates them.

Closely associated with this idea is the "astral projection" theory. This theory states that a kind of mental telepathy occurs in which events that happen miles away appear to happen in front of you. Most of us can think of a time when we were thinking strongly about someone, and suddenly they called, or wrote a letter. Perhaps when we think about a certain place where we once lived, we are actually "haunting" that place at that very moment. Our imagination places us in our childhood home, and if the image is strong enough, the current resident sees our figure walking down the hall. This telepathy might continue even after our death, which would account for the various "historical" hauntings.

There are other theories about the occurrence of apparitions. These include the idea that forces build themselves up, and then are released every so often and are seen as ghosts. There is the theory of subconscious patterns projected by the viewer, of astral bodies and other theories. Most libraries and bookstores are filled with books on the theories of ghosts.

No attempt has been made to explain the stories in

## A Guide to the Ghosts of Lincoln

this book. Instead, they are presented for your interpretation. However, where there is strong historical data it has been included as part of the reporting.

These stories came from a variety of sources.

Many were gathered over the past several years from people who have written and shared their information. For the most part only stories that several people reported have been used. In a few cases a particularly intense single source was used.

Secondary sources were used for other stories. These sources included newspaper clippings and interviews with secondary witnesses. The primary source for these events was sufficiently documented at the time to be considered a strong case.

Finally, in one case, the source was a direct participation. I have visited all but one of the locations.

The names of many of the participants have been changed to protect their rights of privacy. Likewise, the location of the private dwellings are only given in general terms. This is to protect the rights of the people who live in these locations. This book is intended as a general survey of the haunted sites of eastern Nebraska.

If you have information concerning any of these stories, or have knowledge of other locations not included in this book, please write to the publisher at the address opposite the title page.

Linda Wacholder's careful reading of the manuscript was critical in the completion of this work, as was her encouragement and understanding during its late-hour

# A Guide to the Ghosts of Lincoln

manifestations.

The recording of ghost stories is not an idle occupation. Mark Twain, Edgar Allen Poe, Robert Burns, Joaquin Miller and countless other great writers have attempted to define the vague wisps of shapes that haunt them. It is because of their inspiration that I have humbly attempted to exorcise the ghosts of my own past.

# The C. C. White Building Ghost

Of all the events reported in the Lincoln area, perhaps none is more famous, or is as widely accepted, as the apparition at the old C. C. White Building on the Wesleyan University campus. There have been many versions of this story circulated. Here are the facts:

Miss Mary Allen Smith, a music teacher at Wesleyan from 1895 until her death in 1920, is claimed by some to have died in the C.C. White Building. Although there is evidence to suggest that this is the true spirit of the building, the following story has gained popular support.

In 1912 another woman began to work at the music department. Miss Urania Clara Mills taught piano and ear training and became head of the music theory department. She lived in a house in the 400 block of E. 16th in University Place and later at the St. Charles Apartments at 4717 Baldwin.

Apparently Miss Mills was well liked, but many people considered her a frail woman who kept mostly to herself. In the 1915 Wesleyan yearbook there is a photograph of her above a caption which reads, "A daughter of the gods, thou art—Divinely tall and most divinely fair."

There are two common stories concerning the death of

# A Guide to the Ghosts of Lincoln

Urania Clara Mills. One story is that on a spring morning she was seen walking to her office in the C.C. White building. A strong, cool wind was blowing that morning. At 9 a.m. a student entered her office and found her dead.

The other story of her death is quite similar, except that instead of a spring morning with a cold wind, Miss Mills had pushed her way to the building through a late winter blizzard of blowing snow. The blizzard had cancelled classes. It was a Friday morning. When school had reopened the following Monday, her body was found in an office. It was said that she had died of fright.

Miss Mills was about sixty years old when she died. Dates of her death vary, but the most likely is April 12, 1940.

If there were unusual events during the next 18 years, their records have not survived. The C.C. White Building continued to be used as the music building by hundreds of students and faculty with no unusual events recorded. The building remained just an older building on campus for nearly two decades.

All of that changed drastically on Thursday, October 3, 1963.

At 8:50 that morning Mrs. Coleen Buterbaugh walked across the Wesleyan campus on an errand for her boss. She had been sent to find Thomas McCourt, a visiting lecturer from Scotland. He had been assigned an office on the second floor of C.C. White.

Mrs. Buterbaugh strolled through the busy halls of the music department. She later recalled hearing the sound of a marimba playing and the noise of students

# A Guide to the Ghosts of Lincoln

changing classes.

Thomas McCourt, the professor from Scotland, had been assigned the two-room office that had once belonged to Urania Clara Mills. Mrs. Buterbaugh stepped through the open door. The sound of music and the sounds of the students in the hallway ceased as she entered the room.

"I took about two steps into the room and a very strong odor hit me," she said. It was a stale, musty odor. . . "as if someone had turned on a gas jet and let the odor escape."

The smell made her stop suddenly. She became intensely aware of the deathly stillness of the room and of the hallways outside.

I had a strange feeling that I was not in the office alone," she said. "I looked up and for what must have been just a few seconds, I saw the figure of a woman standing with her back to me at a cabinet. She was in the second office. She was reaching up into one of the drawers."

Mrs. Buterbaugh described the apparition as a very tall, slender woman with black silky hair tied back in a bun. Her ankle-length skirt was brown.

Mrs. Buterbaugh felt that the image of the woman was not the only one in the room. She felt the distinct presence of a man sitting at a desk to her left. She turned abruptly, certain that she would see him sitting there. The desk was empty.

Then Mrs. Buterbaugh experienced a phenomenon that she would never forget.

"I looked out the large window behind the desk and noticed that the scenery appeared to be that of many

# A Guide to the Ghosts of Lincoln

years ago. There were no streets and the Willard Sorority Hall that now stands just across the lawn was not there." Mrs. Buterbaugh paused. "Nothing outside was modern."

To look up from a journey into the past and hope to see the world as you know it, and to see instead the streetless open prairies of an age long past, could change your life.

Mrs. Buterbaugh ran from the room. For the next several hours she could not work. She could not dismiss what she had seen as simply her imagination playing tricks on her. She had seen those things, and with her own eyes.

She went to her boss, the Academic Dean, Sam Dahl.

The Dean listened to her story and could see that she was telling the truth. Her skin was white, but she spoke clearly and earnestly. "I didn't dismiss her story," he said. Instead, he led her to other members of the staff.

One of the first they contacted was the visiting professor, Thomas McCourt. McCourt was familiar with such stories, his native Scotland ripe with visitations from the past. He accepted the story without question.

Thomas McCourt returned to Scotland and died a few years later on April 12, the anniversary of the date Urania Mills is believed to have died.

Next, Dean Dahl led Mrs. Buterbaugh to a social science instructor who had worked at the University since the early 1900s.

Together they rummaged through the old yearbooks until the instructor came across a photograph of the woman he remembered best fit Mrs. Buterbaugh's description. Together they identified Miss Urania Mills. The instructor recalled that Miss Mills had been very tall.

Luckily, everyone who heard Mrs. Buterbaugh's story took her seriously. No one laughed the story off. Dean Dahl recalled later that when Mrs. Buterbaugh had first come to see him she was shaking and as white as a sheet. He had never before or since seen anyone in her condition.

Mrs. Buterbaugh was never quite the same. She left her job at Wesleyan, some have said as a direct result of the incident, and moved from Lincoln. For a while she lived in Colorado, but her current whereabouts are unknown.

As for Dean Dahl, to this day the kindly and sincere man holds this incident as one of the most significant of his life.

The particular strength of this story has led institutions and individuals to investigate the events. It was claimed that the Menniger Institute of Topeka interviewed Mrs. Buterbaugh and studied the story. However, no record of this investigation can be found.

Before the building was destroyed, psychics traveled hundreds of miles to see if they could visualize the spirit in the old music building. Many noted that there was a female spirit active in the building, but that the greater power was that of the "man" Mrs. Buterbaugh felt "sitting" behind the desk. This man remains a mystery today.

During the next ten years many events were reported in the C.C. White Building. There were incidents of lights coming on in the middle of the night. Of footsteps in the large hallways of the second floor. And one well-documented story of piano music coming from the small theater in the basement. The music ended abruptly when the door of the theater

# A Guide to the Ghosts of Lincoln

was opened by the group who went to investigate the sound. The fingerboard of the piano on the stage was closed.

One incident concerned some trouble students had been having with various amplifiers and broadcast equipment. It seemed that every time the equipment was left alone for just a few moments, someone would sneak in and turn all the volume switches down. They had to be reset before the project could continue. One evening in 1969, a student who was working with the equipment decided he would try and catch the prankster. He sprinkled the floor with baby powder and then dimmed the lights. He left the building for about an hour. He planned on returning and tracking the culprit by the white footprints from the baby powder.

When he returned all of the sound equipment had been turned down, but the baby powder spread out on the floor about the equipment was undisturbed. The student found it impossible to reach the equipment without tracking the powder himself.

Other minor stories about the building circulated. Stories about "cold spots" on the north stairway, and in the hallway. Faint laughter. Strange smells.

All of the stories from the building came to an abrupt end when the C.C. White Building was demolished in May and June of 1973, just months before the tenth anniversary of Mrs. Buterbaugh's journey into the past.

In the years since there have been no incidents reported in the new administration building that took the C.C. White Building's place; however, there is more than a little evidence that the spirit is still quite active.

# A Guide to the Ghosts of Lincoln

There have been seven reports of strange and unusual events at the address of Miss Mills' apartment. In 1985 several people saw what appeared to be a tall woman dressed in a long dark dress, with her hair tied back. She strolled quickly in front of the apartment building on a night in late April. Several people have begun celebrating Miss Mills' birthday in hopes of seeing something reappear from the past. There have been reports of music being heard by people passing by trees in certain areas around the campus. Often a strange odor can be smelled in the area where the old building once stood.

Perhaps the most notable story is that of a young girl who saw a tall woman standing near the Vance Rodgers Art Center on the Wesleyan campus. She looked "old fashioned," according to the young girl. The girl spoke to the apparition, but it did not answer. When she returned with her mother, the spirit had vanished. The girl was extremely frightened and would not return to the area unless someone was with her.

Still, some instructors who worked on the campus in 1963 when Mrs. Buterbaugh saw the apparition claim that she had actually seen the spirit of Mary Allen Smith. This would have made a more realistic setting for the view of the prairies that Mrs. Buterbaugh saw from the window.

Little research has been conducted into Mary Allen Smith's story. In fact, many interesting questions remain about Mrs. Buterbaugh's sighting and the strange happenings at Wesleyan.

It is difficult to separate fact from myth now that the story has entered the mythology of the city. Still, in the minds of

## A Guide to the Ghosts of Lincoln

people like Dean Sam Dahl, the haunting of the C.C. White Building will always remain one of the great mysteries of the open plains.

# The Sailor

It is like a bad joke. Vicki Reed has lived in the house for a number of years. It is a nice, family-style home near 26th and Sumner. Her husband, now a retired local businessman, had purchased the house in 1964, and Vicki has put a lot of time into making it the kind of home she has always wanted. In the springtime there are flowers around the yard, a fruit tree in the backyard and the lawn is neat and tidy.

One place she is proud of is the dining room. When they had first moved in the room was dark and somber. It had only a small window, really too high to be of any use, which looked out onto the backyard through a tangle of an old lilac bush.

What she had done first was cut down the lilac bush. She hated to do it. The thick wooden trunk and spreading branches had been there a long, long while; from the looks of things, maybe even longer then the house itself. And the sight and smell of those sky-blue flowers were a part of the spring's magic. They reminded her of her childhood. They reminded her of how, on her father's farm near Fremont, the blooming of the lilac hedge heralded the end of winter and the start of the days she would be able to spend her time out-of-doors.

# A Guide to the Ghosts of Lincoln

But cutting the hedge allowed more light to come into the dark dining room. Vicki and her husband made more plans, as homeowners always do, about how they would make improvements to the house.

However, it wasn't until 1979 that they finally did something more about the dining room. That year they hired a contractor by the name of Penrod to remodel the room. First Penrod widened the doorway between the dining room and the adjoining room. A countertop replaced the solid wall between the dining room and the kitchen, and finally, with a great deal of dust and noise, Penrod began to tear down the outside wall to the backyard.

The house is a typical one for this area of town. Built in the early years of this century, it is a modest-sized, wood-framed structure surrounded by other family homes. Nothing overtly unusual or even faintly spooky about the place.

Until the afternoon Penrod came to Vicki.

"Excuse me," he said, "I thought you might want to see this."

Vicki was outside since the dust from the old plaster wall choked the air inside the house. "What?" she said.

Penrod motioned for her to follow. "In the wall," he said. "Something. . ."

She followed him into the house. He went into the dining room. The floor was covered with a large sheet of plastic that did not begin to contain the dust and scraps of wood from the work.

Vicki could still make out the small window which had once been the room's only opening to the outside, but now

## A Guide to the Ghosts of Lincoln

it was widened to almost the size of a wide door. The rest of the wall was stripped to various stages of demolition. In some places the old wood and plaster lathing was exposed, in others the skeleton of the framing was visible.

Penrod was standing at a spot where the wall's framing members stood in exposed rows. "Here," he said, "have a look at this."

Vicki moved to the wall, carefully watching where she put her feet so as to avoid stepping on any of the old rusting nails she saw everywhere.

She squinted to where he pointed. "I don't see anything."

He moved his fingers closer. "There," he said. "It's hard to see. The writing."

She leaned forward. On a particularly smooth bit of ancient plaster she could make out the faint lines of handwriting. The words were in pencil, or faded charcoal. "What. . . ?" she began.

"It's a name, I think," Penrod said. "And something else. . ."

Vicki studied the markings. Indeed, it appeared to be a signature, although she would have to have better lighting in order to make out the name itself...and there, that was certainly a date: April 15, 1912. Then, something else. In Greek, or Latin. *Titan quibus te deum. . .* Yes, it must be in Latin.

She stood up intending to reprimand Penrod for spending his time studying the wall close enough to see such faint scribblings—after all, she was paying him by the hour—when suddenly an overwhelming blanket of terror covered her. She

# A Guide to the Ghosts of Lincoln

stumbled back away from the wall. The empty and open room was deathly quiet.

She turned toward Penrod. He was staring frantically around the room. He sensed it too. His hand was raised as if to quiet her.

A small strip of plaster, hanging on the wall by a thread, began to sway. A corner of the plastic floor covering lifted.

Vicki did not feel the breeze, but the air around her grew stiffling. It was heavy and musty, and beneath that a faint hint of the smell of salt water and the sea.

Then something happened which, had it not beeen repeated over and over again in the coming years, she would have denied experiencing. The room shuddered. A small jolt, as if a gigantic ship had struck some obstruction, passed through the floor. It caused her to throw out her hand for support, and then it was over, leaving her slightly unsure of the steadiness of her legs.

Penrod turned on his heels and marched for the door. "I'm taking off for lunch now," he said. "I'm going."

Slowly, confused, and curious more than afraid, Vicki walked from the room toward the kitchen.

She didn't say much to her husband that night as they ate dinner off paper plates on the floor of their living room. She didn't even say much to him about feeling the shudder in the floor when later she took him into the room and showed him the handwriting, she simply mentioned that she had felt a strange feeling when the carpenter Penrod showed her the writing.

"What do you mean, 'strange'?" he asked. He was look-

# A Guide to the Ghosts of Lincoln

ing around the room.

"Like there was someone. . . " she started.

"How much are we paying this guy?" her husband cut in. "He sure seems to be moving slowly with this thing. Look at all of this. . . "

So she let it ride, for then. In two months the new dining room was finished and the wall where the writing had been was now a large window, and a set of French doors that opened out into the backyard.

One day, about two months after the construction had been completed, Vicki fixed a surprise dinner for her husband. He had worked late and had a lot on his mind from his job.

She carried the place settings into the dining room, placed them on the table and looked up.

The man stood just outside the large window and was looking in at her, and for a moment his appearance did not even frighten her. He somehow seemed to be there, she somehow expected to look up and see him.

He wore dark blue clothes and the kind of cap with a small brim that Vicki later realized sailors of long ago might have worn.

But at that instant she was not thinking much of anything. Only a faint surprise that a man should be standing so close to her window. A half a second later, however, she jerked upright and jumped away from the figure on the opposite side of the glass.

And then she looked, and he was gone.

And then she grew frightened.

The Sailor, as they would come to call him, had made his

## A Guide to the Ghosts of Lincoln

first showing.

As might be expected, Vicki's husband was skeptical. But without even mentioning the eerie feeling she had gotten, he was the one to bring up a spirit.

"Maybe he was a ghost," he said, only half joking.

Vicki said nothing, but two months later when her husband was working in the yard and he looked up to see an old man in a sailor's cap walk past the inside of the dining room window, he no longer joked.

What is the explanation? How to explain that for the past seven years Vicki and her husband have seen the Sailor over a dozen times. How to explain it? Vicki doesn't try to tell it to her friends anymore. At first they were interested and curious about the sightings, but after learning that Vicki saw the man time and time again, her friends would start to cough, tap their feet and try to change the subject. It seemed as though it was all right to see a ghost once, but that the constant reappearance of the apparition made it somehow less real and made her somehow more strange to her friends.

The Sailor is still there. Without a hint, someone will look through the window and there he will be, staring back at them. They have tried to run to the door and see him, but by the time they reach it, he has disappeared. If they simply stand and stare at him, the Sailor evaporates. His entire being fades and then shrinks into nothingness.

Vicki seldom talks about it at all anymore, but when she does her jaw is set tight and her eyes dance as she speaks, replaying every motion of the latest time the faint vapor of the Sailor has paused at her window.

# A Woman in the Fields
# The Spirit at Antelope Park

"I didn't think it was that unusual when it happened the first time," Curt Williams said as he lit his third cigarette. "But what really got me was when we saw it run across the field."

Curt Williams and his fiancee Gay White had a special place where they would go to talk, or simply walk alone and enjoy the fresh summer evenings.

"We haven't been back there since that night," Gay said, fingering the edge of her jacket. "I don't care if I never see that place again."

"Oh, I don't know," Curt sucked on the new cigarette. "I wouldn't mind trying to look for it. It never hurt us, you know."

Gay simply shook her head. "You go there by yourself," she said. "You're not going to get me to set foot in that park."

The first time Curt and Gay met the spirit of Antelope Park was on a June evening shortly after sunset. Like many others, they had heard the stories of a woman who had been seen

# A Guide to the Ghosts of Lincoln

darting across the parking lot and into the fields at the south end of the Pavilion. Like many others, Curt had always considered those stories to be nothing more than a joke, or the results of someone's overactive imagination.

But Curt hadn't been thinking about the stories that June evening.

"I parked the car just to the rear of the caretaker's house and turned off the lights," he said. "The instant that the died out I saw some bushes kind of move."

"We both saw the thing in the bushes," Gay said.

Curt looked at her a moment and then went on. "We didn't see anything then, just the bushes moving."

They got out of the car and locked the doors. Gay had felt a bit chilly and they opened the trunk of the car in order to get a blanket to take along as they walked.

They walked east, between the Pavilion and the caretaker's house. It was just before they reached the edge of the golf course that Gay fell.

"I was walking along and then suddenly I felt my foot slip into a hole. It was a hole in the ground, but I swear I didn't see it," she said. "From the way it felt I guess it must have been about a foot wide and maybe a foot deep."

"I think she just tripped," Curt said. "I'm not sure about this part."

"I am. It was a hole in the ground," Gay insisted. "I felt it. It was like where a post had been or something. Anyway, I fell and twisted my ankle. It didn't hurt too much, but the grass was wet and I got a chill."

"There wasn't any hole in the ground," Curt said. "At

# A Guide to the Ghosts of Lincoln

least none that I could find. Are you sure you didn't trip?"

"We've been over this," Gay said. "There was a hole. I know there was."

In a moment they continued to move on. It had not been a good time for the two of them. They had been going though a rough time as a couple and part of that evening had been spent in an argument. The park had been a place where they thought they could go and calm down. Or, if that failed, at least the darkness might hide some of the anger in their eyes.

"We weren't having one of our best nights," Curt explained. He looked over at Gay. "Remember that, honey?"

Gay now glared at him, but remained silent.

"Anyway," Curt went on, "we had been talking and something I said upset Gay, so she ran off ahead."

"Do you remember what you said?" Gay asked.

"I didn't want her to think I was especially concerned, so I sort of walked in another directon," Curt said.

"You said that if I didn't shut up, you were going to hit me."

"I figured that she could make her way back to the car if we couldn't find one another," Curt continued.

He flicked the ash from the end of his cigarette into a well-used ashtray and looked up. "I walked around for, oh, maybe five minutes. It was a dark night and there were no clouds and no moon. I was standing near a small pine tree of some kind when I heard Gay call my name, nothing else. It sounded like it was coming from the other end of this open area. I walked across that field when I heard her call me again. This time it came from near some bushes."

## A Guide to the Ghosts of Lincoln

He inhaled on the cigarette and held the smoke in a long while before he went on. "I walked toward the bushes and I heard the voice again. This time it sounded like it was about a foot away. She just said my name. . .'Curt.' That was all. I walked around to the other side of the bushes and there was Gay."

Gay had hidden behind the bushes and had wrapped herself in the blanket to ward off the chill.

"I never called him," Gay said. "I was going to hide from him and make him worry. I never said a word."

"Then what?" Curt turned toward her, the smoke curling in front of his eyes. He squinted at her through the smoke.

"We stood there arguing about whether or not I had called you," she said. "You insisted that it was me who was calling your name."

It was then that something caught their attention. It was back across the field, toward the little pine tree. They both saw it.

"It was a woman, that's for sure," Curt said.

"She had on a shawl of some sort," Gay added. "She was running, but her feet didn't touch the ground. She kind of floated above it. It was as if there was a faint light that made her entire body glow. She never looked at me, but just glided across that open area."

They remembered how the night seemed particularly still just then. Even the crickets seemed to have stopped.

"That's when I got spooked," Curt said, lighting yet another cigarette. "It was like it was swimming in the air, the way it went across that field. I mean, it didn't seem connected with the ground. It must have been about twenty yards from us. No further."

"Was it that close?" Gay asked. "I don't think it was that close, was it?"

"Sure it was, honey," Curt said. "It was about fifty feet away when I first saw it. Remember? I said, 'Who's that?' and then it started to move away. That was about twenty yards."

Gay had started to finger her jacket again. "Anyway," she said, "I don't care if I never go back to that park again."

"Oh, we will," Curt said. "I want us to. But maybe in the daytime."

# A Cold Sidewalk and a Typical Lincoln Home

## Two Hauntings off Washington Street

On an evening in late winter in the early days of this century a young man went out for a stroll on South 20th Street. He often chose 20th Street for his walks. Perhaps he liked the feel of the houses. Each had an individuality and character of its own. From dark sandstone castles and stately mansions to green-trimmed and warm family homes, the houses along this street even today speak to the passers-by.

Other streets in the neighborhood were friendly enough, but the houses there seemed to mimic one another. Perhaps he simply liked the trees that lined the street.

We will never know. Nor will we know if he felt a strange premonition that night as he approached the intersection of 20th and Washington.

He stood on the southeast corner of the intersection and

# A Guide to the Ghosts of Lincoln

paused. Maybe he felt a tingling at the base of his soul, a warning that he would never heed; or maybe he simply paused to look about at the houses.

A roadster sped north on 20th from the direction the young man had come. There is no doubt that he must have heard the roaring engine as it approached him. We can assume he might have been curious as to why the vehicle was not slowing down for the intersection.

The car squealed to a stop just in front of the young man. Witnesses disagree as to whether there was one or two people inside the car. The car seemed to pause long enough to identify the young man standing on the corner. Just before the bullets struck him, it appeared as if the young man made a motion as if to turn and run.

As the gunfire still reverberated in the quiet neighborhood, the car sped away into the growing darkness. When the first witness reached the man he was drawing aimless figures onto the sidewalk with his own blood. Moments later he was dead.

This mystery remains one of Lincoln's unsolved murder cases. Although it appeared as if the murderer, or murderers, made certain of the identification of their victim, no motive for the killing was ever ascertained. And, although there were witnesses, no positive identification of the vehicle was made.

Now, decades later, anyone can stand in the exact spot near the intersection and watch as couples, children and friendly neighborhood widows pass by. A surprising number of people, it will be noticed, choose not to walk on the side of the street that would force them to cross the southeast corner.

## A Guide to the Ghosts of Lincoln

Approach it yourself, especially from the south, and you will agree that something urges you to take a different route. Some omen of the past seems to push you away from the corner.

No reports of sightings of an apparition have occurred at this intersection; however, a surprising number of people will claim they "feel something" when approaching the spot. Many people will correctly choose the location when asked to inspect each corner and pick the one where they feel the brutal murder took place.

Within two-and-a-half blocks of this intersection is another of Lincoln's lesser known "haunted houses."

Although older than many of the new apartments that push up to its backyard, the house is of no particularly unusual design. From the porch there is a view of a market. And, if one stands on that porch to view the market, they will feel their backsides grow perceptibly cooler. Other witnesses report feeling a tingling in their ears.

This should not be surprising, for this is the house that talks. On seven separate occasions in since 1983 the occupants have heard voices coming from a location in the front of the house. Although the voice is distinct, no words can be distinguished. It has been described variously as a moan or a sobbing.

The voices seem to originate near the front entry. However, when a precise location is just about made, the voices either cease or seem to move so that they originate a few feet farther away.

## A Guide to the Ghosts of Lincoln

Fortunately, there is a bit of neighborhood history about this house. Many longtime area residents can recall stories of the house being haunted for a number of years.

One resident claimed that the house was originally occupied by a childless couple. After the man died, the woman remained in the house until her death. She was quite old at the time of her death, and lived alone.

There was no family, and no will. The house remained vacant for a number of years. During the 1950s the house was empty. During that time the house took on an ominous appearance—the yard was overgrown with brambles and rose bushes gone wild. The faded and peeling grey paint added to the feeling of mystery.

Several neighbors can recall when children would gather in a nearby alley and dare one another to touch the relatively inviting front door. This may be significant since the back door should have been the much more frightening dare.

The house then became a rental. Not much was done to improve it and a large number of renters moved in and out until the house was purchased again in the 1970s.

Since then there have been three families who have lived in the house. The residents in 1981 lived there for five years, the longest anyone had occupied the house.

Those owners repainted the house and worked the yard back into some semblance of its original beauty. Even then, however, neighborhood children still approached the house with caution.

The final owners of the house refused to provide any additional information, but claimed that voices still did mum-

## A Guide to the Ghosts of Lincoln

ble near the front door. No other manifestations had been reported, although the woman claimed that she made out the word "Sue" or perhaps "some" in the soft sad mumblings of the old talking house.

In the early 1980s the house was torn down in order to build yet another apartment complex. In most hauntings, such destruction also means the end of the apparitions, but not in this case. According to the owner of the apartment complex, the apartment which occupies the spot of the old house is the only unit he has trouble renting.

"The last people only stayed a month," he said. "They claimed the place was haunted."

# Willa Cather and a Ghost Dog

Marty Aiken grew up in a house just down the street from the location of Lincoln's only known ghost dog.

The Aiken house itself, a huge older home, has had its own share of visitors.

"Our house had a pretty interesting history," Aiken, now a lawyer in Austin, Texas wrote. "The house belonged to a long line of famous Lincolnites. The Louis Pound family lived in the house for a while. Before that it was owned by one of the city's founders."

The house was built and stood for years on a corner lot near downtown Lincoln, but was moved to its present location on Van Dorn in the 1940s.

"I suppose the most famous person to have lived in the house was Willa Cather," Aiken continued. "She stayed in an upstairs bedroom for a time while she was attending the University of Nebraska."

Probably Nebraska's best known and most widely read author, Cather attended the University at the turn of the century. The house has a certain literary significance as it was here that she wrote some of her earliest short stories, and many of the poems published in her first book *April Twilights*.

## A Guide to the Ghosts of Lincoln

"I really wanted to write to you about the dog," Aiken continued, "but I should mention that our house wasn't untouched by strange events." While Aiken was growing up his family almost got used to the noises which came from the upstairs bedrooms.

"It would be especially evident when there was a lot of commotion in the house," he wrote. "If we were having a party, or if we were simply loud enough, you could start to hear other noises coming from somewhere on the upper floors."

If there was a lot of activity in the house, someone would inevitably notice a thumping noise coming from above.

"We never really called this a ghost," Aiken explained, "but looking back on this and the other things that went on in that house, I now realize we were probably dealing with what many people call a spirit."

The "other things" that went on in that house were the sounds of items being scraped across the floor, books disappearing and then reappearing in odd and unusual places, and the faint muffled sounds of barely distinguishable voices.

"The voices were strange. You could hear them every once in a while, especially when it was quiet in the house. You could never quite make out the words, however."

Aiken has his own theory about the house. "I like to think the place was haunted by the spirit of Willa Cather. I love to think I grew up with her watching us."

## A Guide to the Ghosts of Lincoln

In those days the Aiken household did not give much thought to the various thumpings, scrapings and lost books. It was simple: all of it was explained away as the creaks and groans of the old house still settling onto its new foundation. The far away voices were nothing more than the wind through rafters somewhere high in the attic.

"We never talked about it all that much," Aiken wrote, "but then just a week ago I talked to my brother on the phone and somehow the subject of ghosts in Lincoln came up."

To each of their surprise, both had remembered the events in the old house, and both had long ago decided it was due to something other worldly. Neither one had ever mentioned it to the other.

"So as we got to talking, we remembered more and more. Then we remembered the dog."

The dog. That dog. The Ghost Dog. People have different names for it, but to this day, many people in the neighborhood know exactly what you are talking about.

"It always would scare you half out of your wits," Aiken continued. "You'd never see it in full daylight, just at night. I had a paper route and the thing would appear when I rode my bike past the house before daylight."

The Thing.

"Sure, there's a dog there," said a ten year old girl from the neighborhood in the summer of 1987. "It is always in that yard. Scary thing. I only see it at night.

# A Guide to the Ghosts of Lincoln

I never go on that side of the street."

The house where the dog appears is just a few houses south off Van Dorn on the west side of a numbered street.

The family who currently lives in the house does not own a dog.

"It was a small dog," Aiken wrote, "but fierce and mean. It would race out of the shadows and be at your heels before it started to bark. I was pretty used to having dogs chase me, but this thing always scared me half to death because it was always in the shadows."

This Thing.

"That's the funny part," said the ten year old. "No one knows where it comes from, or where it belongs. I've seen it a few times. Once it was Halloween. Another time was when all the electricity was off in the city. The entire street was dark."

That time she was not alone.

"A friend and I were walking home from playing at Irving (the near-by Jr. High School). I wasn't even thinking about the dog and I walked down that side of the street. Then, there it was right behind us. It just was there all of a sudden. We both ran."

The dog has never been described by anyone with great detail. It is a medium to small sized dog, light in color, but not white. It is never easy to see, and it never appears unless it has taken the person completely by surprise. It has never been seen in any other location except for the yard of this fairly modern and modest home.

# A Guide to the Ghosts of Lincoln

Once it appears it never goes beyond the property line, and it always retreats suddenly back into the shadows of the yard.

It isn't as if it is defending the house, but it seems more likely that it is mad with fear.

"The creepy thing was," Aiken wrote, "that this dog was extremely nervous. If you had the courage to stop and turn toward it, it stopped and backed away into the darkness. I never could get a good view of it."

Once, however, Aiken did get a glance. He remembers the dog's eyes glowing large and white, just before it disappeared back toward the house.

"The saddest thing about all of this," wrote Aiken, "is that this is all real. There was a tragedy there once, many years ago. A great tragedy many people in Lincoln would recall. It was a sad thing, a very sad thing that happened."

He would not elaborate, but he did add, "I think the dog remembers what happened.

"I am not convinced that there are such things as ghosts, even yet. Perhaps it was just some neighborhood dog. You know some dogs live wild, even in the city," Aiken wrote. "But if there are ghosts, then it wouldn't surprise me that it haunts *that* house."

So in this three block stretch of quiet Van Dorn street there are the literary echoes of Willa Cather and the never stilled fears of a once happy family dog.

Feel free to stroll about this neighborhood one evening and see if you too might not meet up with these

## A Guide to the Ghosts of Lincoln

famous and infamous wisps of the local history, but if you do, be sure that you are on your guard and do not go gentle into that good night.

# The Penitentiary Field

From the safety of his Volkswagen Bug, John noticed nothing but the small shrubs of trees in the dim winter sunlight. To his left the leafless box elder tree was like black lace against the snow-covered field.

"What are you talking about?" John asked.

Roger was pointing frantically to his left. "Right over there. Do you see it? Do you see it?"

The heater of the car puffed out its sad excuse for heat, and the motor puttered.

"See what?" John said, squinting into the snow-blanketed field.

Roger was out of the car. He slid down the slight embankment and ran up to the barbed-wire fence.

Reluctantly, John pulled on the brake and hunted amid the clutter in the back seat for his gloves. It was one of those bitter cold midwestern days. As he stepped out of the small car he could feel the hairs of his nostrils turn stiff in the cold air. But he did smell a curious odor. It was the smell of something decomposing. A smell of something that had nearly rotted away into nothingness. But this was the middle of winter, how could. . . ?

"It went through this fence!" Roger was searching

# A Guide to the Ghosts of Lincoln

madly in the snow, peering at the ground and moving in frantic, excited circles; like a hunting dog picking up a new scent.

John was used to his friend's strange behaviors, but even this was a bit too much. It had to be at least 20 degrees below zero. Roger had insisted they travel south of town on one of the coldest days of the year, over streets packed with ice and snow, to look for a spirit in the middle of an abandoned corn field.

"Roger," John began. He did not finish. Roger raced up to him and began to gesture wildly with his hands.

"Do you mean you didn't see that?" he shouted.

John shrugged. "That cloud of snow carried by the wind. . . ?"

"That wasn't a cloud of snow. It was in the shape of a human being!" Roger ran back to the fence. "It was standing right here when I got out of the car." He pointed to an unblemished section of snow. "It faced me and then turned and slowly walked right through the fence."

John moved to the fence. He studied his friend. He could tell that Roger was serious. As he watched Roger, the strange odor filled the air again. "Can you smell that?" John asked.

Roger sniffed the air. "Smell? Listen, I saw this. . .this thing walk right through that fence. . . ." Now it was Roger who did not finish. John was pointing to a vague spot in the middle of the field. Roger turned.

## A Guide to the Ghosts of Lincoln

Twenty yards from where they stood, a man gazed back in their direction. He was dressed in a light colored coat that hung well past his knees. His hands were not visible. For several seconds the figure stood, back toward the road. Then he raised his right arm above his head, as if he were about to shake it, or to bring it down abruptly. Instead, the entire visage faded into the air.

"Did you see that?" was all that John could say.

The field where John and Roger stood is often referred to as the "Pen Field" due to its location just south of the State Penitentiary. It is located on a road south and parallel to Saltillo Road, just before it reaches the trees at the southern end of Wilderness Park. There is a small dip in the road. Pen Field is on the north side of the road.

There are several stories that concern this field. The above story is the most recent. It occurred in January of 1982.

But Roger and John are not alone in their adventure.

In 1956 or 1957 a U.F.O. was reported hovering near this field. The report was made by several witnesses who claimed to have seen a pale white object floating above the ground.

Also in the late 1950s several inmates from the Penitentiary refused to go on a work patrol near the field. They claimed that the field had a bad feeling to it.

In the mid 1960s a young couple, who had stopped at the spot for a bit of romancing, ran into something. The woman first sensed something, and then insist-

## A Guide to the Ghosts of Lincoln

ed they drive away from the spot. Next, they both reported noticing an odd smell "like sulfur" or similar to a vague fishy odor. Then, in the darkness in front of them a silver-blue light appeared, moved across the road in front of their car, and disappeared out into the field to the north.

No one who has spent a winter in the open plains of eastern Nebraska needs to be reminded of the bitterness of the season. At times the wind will race out of the Canadian Rockies with a howl that is nearly human. It speeds across hundreds of miles with nothing to slow it down except for the few dead stalks of last year's corn crop.

On January 12, 1888, the day dawned unseasonably balmy. All across the Midwest, children hurried to school as men and women took advantage of the weather to move loads of feed, or to mend fences or work the livestock. In the early afternoon the sky suddenly turned dark. It is estimated that in the next few hours the temperature dropped as much as 60 degrees.

A light wet snow that had been falling turned instantly to thick sheets of ice, pushed by winds of 60 miles per hour. It would be a storm that would be remembered for a century. The Blizzard of '88.

A man who lived just northwest of Roca left his home around four in the afternoon to search for his daughter who had not returned from school. The air was so thick with blowing snow that visibility was reduced to a few feet.

# A Guide to the Ghosts of Lincoln

The man's daughter had remained at school with most of the other students who huddled about the big stove in the middle of the room. In the morning the temperatures were estimated to be about 40 degrees below zero. But the winds had died down and the girl returned home. Shortly after she arrived, her father's horse returned.

They waited for him for another day until they realized that he would never return home. Five months later his body was found in a field, curled in a small ball. The coyotes and wolves had been there first, but it was he. He had been found in a field that matches the location of "Pen Field."

Another story that surrounds this area is that of the unusually brutal murder of a guard from the Penitentiary.

In the 1940s, the story goes, a particularly hated guard was watching over a group of inmates as they worked in a field. Apparently the guard took every advantage of his position to demean and ridicule the prisoners. He was universally hated, and even feared.

At some point that morning he was murdered. It is the common belief that most of the prisdoners were responsible for his death. Parts of his badly mutilated body were never found. The prisoners continued to work in the field until the guard's body was discovered later that day.

There are many other stories that have circulated about this lonely stretch of road, so close to the city limits.

## A Guide to the Ghosts of Lincoln

If there is any doubt about the power of things that move in a world beyond ours, drive out to the edge of this mysterious field and sit awhile in the silence of that strange air.

Perhaps you will then realize the strength of invisible powers.

# A Walking Shadow's Hour Upon the Stage

It was fresh spring morning in 1906. The young carpenter stood high above the ground and surveyed the city. He stood with each foot delicately placed on the roof rafters with nothing but four stories of empty air between the packed clay earth and him.

He felt nearly as tall as the white dome of the State House that dominated the skyline. A cable car clanged in the distance. On the streets of the town horses and carriages moved quickly about the day's business.

At his back was the campus of the University. The young carpenter breathed in the April air. It was a good day to be alive, for he not only worked as a carpenter, but earlier in the year he had started his studies at the University.

His father, however, had not been pleased when the young man told him that he wanted to take classes in drama. There wasn't much future in that, as far as his father could see, unless he planned on becoming a politician or a preacher. There wasn't much of a future in schooling at all, as far as his father could tell. Better stick to being a carpenter.

The young man chuckled at the irony. Here he was,

# A Guide to the Ghosts of Lincoln

standing at the very pinnacle of the new theater building for the University. Directly below him the classrooms were already taking shape as his brothers worked to complete them.

From where he stood in the rafters above the building's attic he felt free and soaring—above them all. He would show them. One day he would perform on a great stage of the city. He would play a great part in some play and his father would stand and cheer with the thousands of others as he calmly took his bows before them.

It was at that moment—poised between heaven and earth, between a certainty of greatness and the sky—that a great fear seized him.

For years the young man had scrambled on the rafters of houses and buildings that his father built in the city with never a thought of the danger. Now, on the tallest building they had worked upon, he felt his legs freeze. He knew he could not make it off the rafters alive.

During a moment that lasted an eternity he could feel himself tipping forward. It took a lifetime for the arc of his body to pass his center of gravity on its path to the ground below. Remotely, from some far away place he could hear someone screaming. The screeching grew until he realized that it was his own voice shattering the air about his ears.

Several people watched his body fall. His brothers and his fathers, on the floors below, looked up at the scream. And, oddly enough, the dean of the drama department

## A Guide to the Ghosts of Lincoln

happened to be passing by. He watched in horror as the boy's body seemed to drift to the ground below.

The dean was the first to reach the body. It lay on the first floor of the building. It struck the dean as odd that there was very little blood and the body lay in what appeared to be a very comfortable position. A small trickle of sawdust continued to drift down from the skeleton of an attic high above.

Shortly after the funeral several unexplained incidents began to occur in the structure that was to be named the Temple Building. Tools of the carpenters and masons began to disappear. His brothers, who continued to work on the building, thought they heard him call to them. At night the sounds of his scream seemed to echo through the half-completed walls.

It has been over 75 years since the young carpenter-actor lost his life during the construction of the Temple Building, but he has yet to disappear.

In the late 1930s a series of events took place that left an impression on more than one drama student:

After a band rehearsal one evening an echo of music filtered through the building.

For a period of several months witnesses claimed to have seen lights dancing about the building at odd hours.

And, as has been the case in several incidents right up to the present day, there were reports of people hearing the sound of something crashing down. The sound is as if a large weight has fallen from a high place.

Dr. Dallas Williams, a long-time professor of speech

## A Guide to the Ghosts of Lincoln

and drama, was convinced that the unexplained events in the Temple Building were the work of the young man who fell to his death during its construction. In his years in the building, Dr. Williams was witness to some unusual events.

"No one can explain why these things happened," he said. "But often after doing a play we would all hear music. It came from nowhere, and yet was distinct, though very soft. We would search the building trying to find a place where the music could originate. We could never find such a place."

After a production of "Marat-Sade" in the late 1960s or early 1970s, a sound echoed through the building. It was described as the sound of a large sandbag falling to the floor. Several people searched the building, fearing that a terrible accident of some kind had happened. No explanation for the crash was found.

The number of events seemed to die down after a bit during the 1970s, but recently, especially after the completion of the remodeling of the Temple Building, the events have increased. Many people who are alone in the building mention that they have heard footsteps that seemed to vibrate through the walls. Lights flicker from the hallways. On a Saturday in June 1982 a loud crash, like the sound of several books hitting the floor, was heard throughout the building. No explanation for the sound was found.

A new sound has been added in the last decade: that of a thumping noise coming from the attic of the building.

High above the classrooms, stage and offices, the Temple Building's attic sits like many of our attics: cluttered with spiderwebs and dust. Through the patches in the floor one can make out the outline of the roof rafters. In the distance the city buildings clutter the skyline. Far below on the stage of the University's theater, actors strut and fret their hour upon the stage and then. . . ?

# A Potpourri

## I. The Warehouse

At first the men joked about it. Working nights alone in the warehouse already created a kind of odd workplace humor. In the darkened building the stereo cabinets, electronic equipment and other goods took on a kind of life of their own. Even throwing on the big, powerful lights didn't help much. The place was still creepy.

But the three men who worked the late shift at the warehouse, loading trucks and unloading crates, kidded one another and created their own kind of code language of familiar jokes and one liners. A stranger walking into the place might believe they had entered a foreign world the way of the three of them spoke to one another.

"Water cooler," Ted shouted out.

"That's my man," Brian responded from somewhere in the back of the huge, open room.

"Weeelll. . ." Curt threw in. He had been working near the tiny door at the back of the building. The nonsensical diologue got them all laughing.

On one such night, when the three of them had just

## A Guide to the Ghosts of Lincoln

finished shouting out a bantering diologue, Curt first saw him. A tall, slender and unassuming man stood in the shadows a good deal away from where Curt was working. He was not watching Curt, although he seemed quite aware of his presence. He was looking down and slightly in the distance.

For some unknown reason, Curt did not say anything to this man. Something told him that the man would not have responded anyway. Instead, he called out to his fellow workers.

"Hey, gentlemen," he shouted. "We are not alone."

There was a pause of silence. Then Brian shot back, 'Yeah, right. Someone out there is watching us."

Curt had already started to move toward Brian's voice. He had turned away from the back door and had lost sight of the mysterious, slender man. There was a growing edge of panic in Curt's voice. "There is someone in the building besides us," he said.

Now Ted came running. "What's going on?" he said when he reached Curt.

"There's someone in the building," Curt said. "There was a man back by the back door."

Ted was the kind of person who never hesitated about anything. "Let's go have a look," he said.

Brian had come up from the front of the warehouse. He grabbed at Ted's arm. "Hold on. What if he has a gun?"

Ted shrugged it off. "Why would anyone carry a gun into a warehouse in the middle of the night?"

# A Guide to the Ghosts of Lincoln

The three of them moved slowly back toward the rear of the warehouse. But as they approached the spot where Curt had first noticed the slender man, even Ted moved slower.

"He was over there," Curt whispered. He pointed.

"He's not there now," Brian whispered back.

"We have a genius among us," Ted said. But even he was keeping his voice down. "No, he's not there now, gentlemen."

"Let's check the back door," Brian said.

Together they moved to the back door. It was bolted from the inside, just as it was supposed to be at this time of night. Ted unbolted it and swung the door wide.

They stepped outside. "O" Street was practically deserted. In the parking lot of the supermarket across the street two cop cars were parked side by side so that the drivers could speak to one another. The engines of the cars threw out low hanging clouds of light blue smoke. A single car waited for the light to change at the intersection of 27th Street.

"No one here," Brian said. They went back inside the warehouse and bolted the door shut behind them.

"How did he get in?" Curt demanded.

Ted shrugged. Brian said nothing.

"Let's spread out and walk through the building," Ted said.

"Right," Curt said. "Let's all spread out and walk through the building so some guy who is hiding with a gun can find us easily."

## A Guide to the Ghosts of Lincoln

"I tell you, he doesn't have a gun," Ted said. "We'll find him if we spread out and kind of walk together in a line."

"You first, John Wayne," Brian said.

But Ted was already making his way behind the crates of unopened stereo speakers. "Just make a lot of noise. Let him know..." Ted had started behind a stack of crates and then stopped. He backed up a step. "All right," he said firmly, "all right. We just want you out of here. No questions. Do you understand? Just stand up so we can watch you leave. That's all we want." Ted moved slowly toward the far end of the warehouse. He glanced over to his two co-workers.

Slowly Curt and Brian moved to join Ted. As they moved toward him they tried to peer over the large crates to see the slender man.

Ted's hand shot into the air. "Ssshhh!!!"

They fell silent, each trying to listen past the beating of their own hearts. There is no such thing as a noiseless warehouse. The slightest sound, no matter what its cause, reflects off the expanse of walls and magnifies, especially at three in the morning. A scampering mouse in the sudden stillness can sound like a horse. The creaking of a heavy wooden crate as it settles can sound like the roar of a jet engine, but what each of them heard, was footsteps echoing near the rear of the building where Curt had first seen the slender man.

They spun around. No one was there.

"I just saw him here," Ted was nervous now, poin-

## A Guide to the Ghosts of Lincoln

ting at a spot nearby. "He was just there, a tall guy, in the darkness. He was standing right there just a minute ago."

No one was ever found in the warehouse, not that night and not the countless other nights over those months in 1986 when the three of them worked together and the events began to multiply like a plague.

Once, a week after Curt had first seen the man, Brian was working in a corner area and had come around a post. Out of the corner of his eye, he caught a movement from the shadows. When he jerked his head toward the movement, he caught a glimpse of a tall figure in a dark coat before it disappeared.

A few weeks later Ted had unpacked an expensive turntable, had taken a coffee break and then returned to find the turntable missing. This was a serious problem, since they were all responsible for everything in the warehouse, and the owner would not tolerate stories of expensive merchandise that "just disappeared." They managed to stall the owner when he asked about it. They tried to figure out a way to explain the missing turntable. One night, when they were just about to give the owner some story about the turntable never being delivered, Brian found it sitting in the middle of the table in the coffee room.

More questions than answers arose. Voices were heard and strange footsteps as if someone was walking on the roof. Shadows moved within shadows. Tensions grew between the formerly friendly workers. Now the night was not broken with laughter and light talk. Instead, the three of them worked in a growing cloak of dark and murky silence.

Ted was the first to quit. He said that he found another job, which was true, but the new job paid less and it was clear out near the airport.

The owner eventually hired an older man to replace Ted. The new man didn't want to have anything to do with stories of haunted warehouses and of figures that appeared and then disappeared. He therefore spent most of his time sitting in the coffee room smoking cigarettes anyway, and Curt and Brian had to work twice as hard to make up for the work he didn't do.

Brian just quit. It became too much like a sweat and toil job and nothing but the too-small paycheck to make it worthwhile.

Curt stayed on until 1987. He worked with the new employees in a stoney silence. Once, during a coffee break, one of the new workers said he had seen something he couldn't explain. He had been stacking empty boxes and had felt that someone was watching him. He had looked up to catch a glimpse of a tall slender man in a dark jacket. Curt said nothing, and stared into his coffee.

Curt was fired not long after that. Equipment was disappearing, and although the owner didn't say anything, Curt knew the owner suspected him.

A short time later the building changed hands and is no longer used as an electronic equipment warehouse.

A Guide to the Ghosts of Lincoln

## II. A Place for the Willies

This is nothing but a place and a time. The place is at the end of a dead end road near the southern end of the huge grain elevators near Van Dorn park. The road grows narrower and narrower until it peters out in a clump of weeds and clumps of Pampers and the styrofoam boxes that once held steaming hot hamburgers.

As for time, there is a bit of a difference. Right now there is nothing there but the Willies. The Willies are those little icy fingers which dance up and down one's spine without warning or explanation. The Willies are there now. They wait for anyone.

At a different time, back in 1956 or '57, there was something else. One evening in early winetr, the story goes, there was something else here.

Lights, some said, freaks of nature, a combination of atmosphere and moisture and air pressure. But others claim that on that night in the late 1950s the lights were more defined, the lights were shapes and those shapes were the first of a long series of sightings of unidentified flying objects. There are those who were there that night and they claim it was a saucer, but their names have been lost to history.

And then there are those still in Nebraska who drove down the lonely road the next day, or the day after and who will tell you that they saw scortched earth and grass,

## A Guide to the Ghosts of Lincoln

places on the land where the vegetation had been vaporized. They will tell you that for years afterwards nothing grew in those circles.

And they will tell you that after the sighting near the grain elevators the Nebraska countryside was dotted with cow mutilations. Farmers began to find dead cows in the fields. Cows that seemed to have no injuries on their bodies, no diseases, but one very odd condition: they had no blood. All of their blood had disappeared.

The UFOlogists will tell you that cow mutilations, scortched earth and other such happenings are nothing unusual. One branch of them will go so far as to claim that alien beings are taking the blood of cattle because it indicates the location of certain minerals in the soil which the space travelers need to save their own race.

Others will point to the well-documented UFO sighting near the west bank of the Platte River on the old highway between Omaha and Lincoln which occurred about the same time.

In this sighting a police, officer stopped by a field in the early morning hours to investigate a strange craft that was glowing. Later, under hypnosis, he told of a vague recollection that some creatures, "that looked like ghosts" took him into the craft.

He found himself standing outside of his patrol car. He felt a bit dazed, and disoriented, but otherwise well. He got back into the car and looked at his watch. He expected the watch to tell him he had been out of his car for about five minutes, but three hours had passed instead.

Because of his confusion, and because he had vague memories of seeing the beings, and knew for certain that he had seen a large craft in the field, the officer volunteered to under-go hypnosis. It was then that the details of the night's events became known.

It was during this same time that the events near the grain elevators took place.

And those who go out in serach of such places, those who find such places by accident, and those who believe that our pride has limited our ability to see that there are indeed other worlds than ours, will tell you that this spot is a special one, a place where the ordinary world is left behind.

And almost everyone who has found the spot along the southern end of the elevators will tell you that stopping there, even for a moment, inevitably brings about an intense feeling of agitation and fear.

# III. The Big House

They have lived in the northeast Lincoln house for 11 years now. It is a big house, 2800 square feet, within two blocks of 52cd and Adams.

## A Guide to the Ghosts of Lincoln

For the young couple the house was a dream house. Eileen Andrews and her husband Ken wanted children and the house was large enough for their planned family. It was that and more.

When their son Benjamin was born they used one of the large bedrooms on the second floor for him. They put up curtains with pictures of trains and animals on them, and filled the room with toys and games and books.

"About the time Benjamin was born and we started to use the room was when I began to smell it," Eileen said. "It was a sickening sweet smell that I often smelled near Benjamin's room, and sometimes in the dining room." Ken and Eileen called in exterminators, thinking it was caused by some kind of pest. They searched around the house for leaking gas or some other explanation. They found nothing, and the smell continued, appearing and disappearing like, well . . .like a ghost.

"The smell is hard to take. I mean it really gets to me sometimes," she said. "I feel real funny talking about this. Most of the time people look at me as if I am crazy when I talk about all of this. It's gotten so I can't even tell my own brothers and sisters about it anymore."

For several years the big house had stood vacant before the Andrews moved in. There was a bit of a clean up chore for them then, but with new paint and the fresh spring air blowing through the windows, the house soon took on a charm and fresness.

Long before that, however, an elderly woman had liv-

## A Guide to the Ghosts of Lincoln

ed alone in the house for many years. The woman kept pretty much to herself. It was said that she had been married some years before, but not much else was known about her.

That much Eileen had learned simply from the neighborhood gossip and history. And no, no one had ever heard of the woman talking about strange smells. . . Did Eileen have trouble maybe with the plumbing, they wanted to know.

For a moment Eileen's voice wavered. The next part was harder to talk about.

"Then, one night while we were watching television I caught a motion out of the corner of my eye. There was one of Benjamin's toys, a plastic alarm clock, sitting on the edge of the television table. I looked at it. It was rocking back and forth, as if someone had just tipped it. I stared at it. It continued to rock for a long time." For the first time, Eileen was afraid.

"But we weren't too paranoid. When something like what has happened to us happens to people you'd be surprised at the way you try to find a rational explanation for things. You just don't want to believe that there is absolutely no normal explanation for what you are seeing."

There was no explanation for what happened next. Eileen and Ken sleep with their bedroom door closed. Ever since Benjamin reached the age of four they got in the habit of closing their door at night. It helps keep the room warm in the cold winters, and cool in those hot,

## A Guide to the Ghosts of Lincoln

locust filled nights of summer.

"We had been asleep for a couple of hours," Eileen said, "when there was a knock on the bedroom door. Two knocks, actually. Just like that: boom, boom. Ken said: 'Benjamin? Is that you?'

"There was no answer. Ken got out of bed. I was suddenly very awake. I remember that the house was dead quiet. It was the kind of quiet I have never experienced before. It was as if there were no noises *anywhere in the world.*"

In that stillness, with her husband standing at the opened and empty bedroom door, they heard the footsteps.

"There was someone walking around in Benjamin's room." Eileen's voice grew quiet and nearly inaudible. "They were heavy, adult footsteps. We both could hear them quiet clearly."

After a moment's hesitation Ken ran from the room. Eileen dashed out of bed and followed him. Benjamin's bedroom door, which was also kept closed, was wide open. The five year old was sitting on the edge of his bed, crying.

"He told us that a man was in his room. He said that a man had walked past his bed."

If it hadn't been for the footsteps they had heard they might have dismissed Benjamin's tears as a bad dream. Instead, they called the police.

"The cops didn't find anything," Eileen said. "They searched the house, the yard, and even the windows. Nothing was disturbed."

## A Guide to the Ghosts of Lincoln

Eileen went on, having told this much, she might as well keep going.

"We kept trying to explain things away, to avoid thinking that the smells, the objects that moved and the footsteps were related. But we couldn't avoid the obvious: something was going on in the house."

Eileen discovered that a man who lived in the neighborhood had actually grown up in the house. She had never met him, but had seen him around the area. She went to his house and introduced herself. He was friendly enough, but as soon as she started to ask about the house he stopped her.

"He said that he didn't want to talk about it. I asked him what he meant and he started to get rude. 'I said I don't want to talk about that house,' he said. I couldn't get a word out of him after that," Eileen said.

She paused. "I thought that the guy in Ben's room might be the end of it," she said. "But now it's gotten worse." There was a long pause.

"One evening about a week ago we had all gone out to a movie. We had been talking about what we saw most of the way home, but when we got here everyone just stopped talking. That was kind of strange all by itself. I even knew, when I opened the front door that something was strange. There was that same deathly silence like the night in Ben's room. And there was the smell.

"Our dining room opens up into the living room. We

# A Guide to the Ghosts of Lincoln

all walked in and then just sort of noticed him."

There was a long, long pause and when she started to speak her voice was cold, foreign and distant. "A man in a red plaid lumberjack coat was walking around the dining room. Just walking around. Ken shouted something at him, but he was absolutely unaware of us. And it was like there was an invisible sheet of foggy glass between us. He made no noise. The air in the room was so thick it swallowed every sound. He moved around the edge of a wall and was gone. . ."

Eileen's voice trailed off. They called the police again, and the police came, searched the area and told them that no one was hiding anywhere in the house and that no one had entered the house while they were gone. They nodded at the police and after they left Eileen cried most of the night.

In spite of all that has happened, and although she is constantly on edge now, Eileen's biggest problem is not the fear of the unknown visitor, but rather her sense of isolation. There is no one who she can talk with about what has happened. Even her best friends grow uncomfortable when she brings up the topic.

"I used to at least say 'Oh I believe in ghosts' when people started talking about the unknown, but I don't even do that anymore. It only means people will ask why I believe, and then, when I tell them, they grow quiet and act strange. They just don't want to hear about it."

Eileen's voice was stronger now. "Sometimes I think

# A Guide to the Ghosts of Lincoln

I am going crazy, but then I *know* what happened, happened. I just don't talk about it much anymore."

# IV. Grandpa

They call him "The Pans," just a nickname he got when he was still quite small, but with his gigantic smile and loving heart the name just sort has stuck with him.

The six year old boy lives in a home near 27th and M street, in an area of older homes and working class Linconites.

He laughs and plays and cries and runs just like any other six year old growing up in a midwestern town. He comes in late for supper, he wants to watch more television than his parents will allow and yet he is thankfully still young enough not to be too embarrassed to give his father or his mother a big kiss in public.

In short, the Pans is a normal child in nearly every way. He watches his Grandpa walking about the house and tells his mother what Grandpa said or did. The only unusual thing is that the boy's grandfather has been dead seven years.

It all started when the boy was still quite small. He

## A Guide to the Ghosts of Lincoln

found a golf ball that belonged to his grandfather. The Pans' mother kept a few of them in an empty match box in the kitchen drawer.

He was less than a year old then, but the boy took to the golf ball as if it were the last toy in the universe. He clung to it night and day, and slept with it next to his pillow at night.

Nothing too unusual about a small child taking to a favorite toy, even though this one was a bit less comforting than a soft teddy bear or a cuddly doll. But soon his mother began to notice other things.

When they took out the family scrapbook the Pans would squeal and point to the photographs of his dead grandfather as if he recognized him.

By the time he was three the Pans was surprising his parents by telling them just exactly what they were thinking. He began to respond to their thoughts as if they had been spoken. "Why do I have to go to sleep now. . . I love you too, Daddy. . . Go to the zoo today? Yes, I want to!"

And now he sees his grandfather walking the rooms of the house. He describes the man to his mother, who has had the good sense to try not to act too surprised when he describes details about her father that only she could know. The Pans will tell her of his little sideways limp, of the way he carefully has combed the few remaining hairs of his balding head back across his head, of the way he throws his arms above his head when he stops to stare out the window, or sits in the big leather chair.

## A Guide to the Ghosts of Lincoln

His parents are looking for someone who knows about these kinds of things. Someone who knows something about why people seem to be able to read minds, about how people can see things that only existed in the past, and about why their small lovely son looks over his shoulder to see a man long since vanished from this earth.

# Shapes in the Fog Around Lake Street Lake

In the early days of Lincoln there had been a farm nearby. It had mainly raised dairy cattle and sold the milk and cream to the growing town a mile or so to the north. No one is sure what happened to that farm. All that is left today is a certain feeling, a spirit of some kind that lingers behind at the lake.

Sitting at the edge of the small lake one can almost imagine what it must have been like years ago. The countryside dips and tilts until it forms a small indentation, which in winter is filled with water. During the day it is peaceful enough, and the modern city dweller can almost picture the dairy cows that grazed here. Or the phantom farmer on his horse, slowly riding out to check on his cows.

There are many stories of the spirit that inhabits the park at 15th and Lake streets. Nearly everyone who has passed by the lake in the dark will comment on a particular feeling. Sometimes that feeling is a positive one, but more often it takes the form of a chill in the air, or one that has worked its way down the observer's spine. There have been times, however, when the feeling has taken much more of a definite shape.

## A Guide to the Ghosts of Lincoln

One of the earliest events happened to no less a personality than the young Loren Eisley. Eisley would grow up to gain fame and world recognition as an anthropologist and gifted writer.

Eisley spent his first seven or eight years in a house near Eighteenth and South streets. At that time, South Street marked the southern edge of the city.

Shortly after his family moved to the location, Eisley made friends with the neighborhood bully, named appropriately "the Rat." Eisley was pressured into entering the dark and fearful sewage tunnels at the edge of Lake Street Lake. Eventually, the dark and foreboding atmosphere of the spot led him to confront the first true fear of his young life.

Since then there have been many other similar stories about Lake Street Lake. The most common comment continues to be the sensation of a chill when approaching the lake. It is often a chill too definite and drastic to be explained by the mere presence of the lake itself.

One might be expected to discover, while strolling on an evening's walk on a clear night, a thick fog surrounding the lake. The fog, which often settles in the indentation, only adds to the eerie feeling.

But there have been other events as well. In 1977 Dick Dutton was on a walk in the evening. It was a cool night and the streets were nearly deserted. Most people were at home near a raging fire. But Dick was restless and liked to walk about to wear off that restlessness, no matter what the weather.

# A Guide to the Ghosts of Lincoln

Usually Dick would not venture past 17th street in his evening walks staying instead close to the parks and streets to the east. But this particular evening he chose to walk west on Lake Street, and past the lake.

He first noticed the foggy air as he approached the small park. This struck him as a bit odd, for the air seemed much too cold for fog.

He had decided to take a leisurely walk about the lake and then return home. As he was about a quarter of the distance around, he heard the distinct sound of rushing water. He paused to try and locate the sound. It was not right that water should be rushing on a night as cold as this was.

He peered through the darkness and the fog and noticed an older man staring back at him from across the lake. The apparition struck Dick as so unusual that for a long moment he didn't speak.

Dick slowly became aware that the man was not looking at him, but rather beyond and through him, to something else in the misty night.

"Pretty cold night, isn't it?" Dick called out to the figure on the other bank. The sound of his own voice cutting through the chill air startled him.

The old man did not change expressions, but slowly and quite distinctly *faded*. The figure did not turn, nor did he walk away, but, according to Dick Dutton, he actually blended into the mist.

A similar event happened on the night of March 21, 1981, to Arthur Hulbert and his wife Jean. They had been out along the lake walking their dog, Snoopy. They often walked her past the lake. Like Dick, the Hulberts first noticed the sound of running water on an otherwise very cold evening. The sky had been clear and there was no mist over the lake.

Both of them noticed the elderly gentleman on the southern bank of the lake, but had not commented on him. Jean was to recall later that the man had "just seemed to disappear," although they had not watched him vanish.

When they had rounded the lake they both noticed that the man no longer stood on the shore. At that point Art mentioned something about the man who had been there. As they approached the spot where the man had been standing, Snoopy began to tug at her leash and try to pull them away from the area. Snoopy was a well-trained dog who was used to being on a leash.

They pulled at her line and finally Snoopy allowed herself to be moved toward the southern bank; however, as they reached the area where they had seen the man, Snoopy began to run wildly in a tight circle. She barked, snarled and snapped at the air.

This behavior was so unusual for Snoopy that Art and Jean began to discuss it. This led to the subject of the old man who had stood at the spot. Neither of them had seen him move away from the lake, and yet he was nowhere to be found. Art remembers feeling a cold draft of "stale" air pass by them then, although neither one had yet begun to talk of anything like a haunting.

## A Guide to the Ghosts of Lincoln

They had to practically drag Snoopy away from the lake.

There are many other stories of this quiet and peaceful park in the southwest corner of the city. None of the people who have witnessed even a minor incident at the lake feel that the spirit is a "bad" spirit. In fact, many people claim to obtain a sudden feeling of peacefulness and relaxation when they visit the park. No one, however, walks away from Lake Street Lake without feeling something.

In the last few years several incidents have been reported of a "blue shimmering shape" running along the creek that feeds Lake Street Lake. The most common place this figure has been seen is at the tail end of Irvingdale Park, just off 17th Street and Harrison Avenue. During the summer of 1987, three individual cases were reported of this wispy figure moving along the creek bed during the dark moonless hours past sunset on hot, summery evenings.

# Robbers' Cave

The entire subsurface of the southwest corner of the city is made of the same porous sandstone that forms Robbers' Cave. Ground water for centuries has creeped its way through the soft rock and formed a vast series of catacombs, with a labyrinth of tunnels that run for miles underground. The tunnels at one time apparently connected the State Hospital with the Penitentiary.

There is only one opening to these caves, and it is known as Robbers' Cave.

Years ago, to visit the cave, the first thing was that you had to get past the old woman and the three snarling coyotes. At the time when Robbers' Cave was first open to the public, she was the woman who owned the land around the entrance, and collected a small entrance fee.

You would knock on the screen door of the old farmhouse and wait. In the window was a crude drawing of a hideous skull and crossbones. The words "fluoridation kills" were scrawled below them.

The door would finally open and the woman would appear. She was a tall woman with a not unpleasant personality. But often she would lean out the door, towering above you and whisper, "There has been no one

## A Guide to the Ghosts of Lincoln

else in the cave today. . .so I'll have to turn on the lights for you."

If it was possible for the lights to be turned on, you always thought, wouldn't it just as possible for those same lights to be shut off while you were deep in the bowels of the cave?

Often she would insist that you look at the three pet coyotes that were her pride and joy. You would follow her behind the house, hoping that the beasts would be caged. And always the coyotes would glance at you with their cold animal eyes, unlike pets, unlike even the meanest steet dogs, and pace nervously in their kennels. They would suddenly stop and howl, their long tails arched stiff and bristly. Their calls seldom echoed into the entrance of the cave.

The entrance to the cave was harmless enough. Just a simple old wooden door with a frame that angled sharply into the ground. If there had been no one else in the cave, the old woman would have to return to the house and get her keys to unlock the padlock on the door. Once inside you always listened to make certain she did not replace the lock.

When the door opened, the first draft of stale, damp air hit you in the face. To enter below the surface of the earth is an uncommon experience. It goes against some basic truth we must all keep inside of us.

A steep staircase led down for the first hundred-and-fifty feet. The old steps were at such an angle that every one was a flirtation with disaster. At the first bend in

# A Guide to the Ghosts of Lincoln

a well-worn path, a glance back up the stairs would reveal the last glimmering of daylight that creeped through the entrance far above.

At first sight of the Well, you knew that the ordinary world of rolling hills and straight streets was behind you. The ground water had seeped into the sandstone to form a massive underground hole that plunged two hundred vertical feet into darkness. A single bulb above the hole barely lit up the small, slender, descending passage and the series of cubbyholes in the Well's wall.

It was here that the bats often hid. High in the cistern ceiling a seething mass of dark fur meant a hundred bats were awake and preparing to fly. They were elsewhere in the caves as well, but they nearly always could be found in the Well.

In an instant they would drop like stones and flutter past your face and into a dark chamber nearby.

Several passages led from the bottom of the Well. One of them was named "fat man's misery" because of the narrow opening between the walls that forced you to scrape your sides on the damp and clammy sandstone.

Other passages curved and wound through the dark chambers. Many had low roofs that constantly dripped water the color of blood. Some of the passages would end against a flat wall where hundreds of initials had been carved, most of them wearing away from the constant drip of water that seeped through the rock.

One passage, however, led through a long tunnel that had nearly straight walls and a flat ceiling and dim yellow bulbs glowed feebly, separated by great expanses of darkness. The lights were your only guide through the eternal night.

There were long stretches along this tunnel where you would walk through nearly total darkness, your eyes straining to see the glow of the next faint bulb. And the bats, with their pinched and creased faces, flew through this passage regularly, turning their sightless eyes and oversized ears within inches of your face as they flew past.

Several small rooms branched off this passage. Most of them were not lit. One particularly invisible one was a small crevice that twisted and widened back on itself. It was called the Question Mark.

At last, after another long descent, the passage opened and the lights became more frequent. The passage turned into a series of moderately sized chambers. From the end of the last of these chambers, an ascending walkway led back to the Well, and eventually back up to the world.

Many visitors to Robbers' Cave quite likely never even saw the chamber called Robbers' Roost. It was easy to pass by, for one had to climb five feet up a series of holes chipped into the wall of the cave. Once up these, a narrow ledge, nearly hidden from the helpful glow of the electric lights, led into the vast chamber, hidden from direct view by a rock face.

Immediately one sensed a difference in this chamber from the rest of the cave. For one thing, this chamber

# A Guide to the Ghosts of Lincoln

was dry. A thick cushion of dry sand covered the floor. The room was nearly a perfect square. On one side there was a firepit, for nature had caused a natural chimney to be created by some long-forgotten collapse of the sandstone. If you dared the spiders and the threats of a thousand bats, you could lean your head far under the firepit, twist your head and see the faintest glimmer of blue sky far above you through the slender chimney.

It was here, according to local legend, that various outlaws hid. One story had Jesse James hiding in the chamber on his trips through Nebraska. Others claimed that Robbers' Roost was a hideout in the underground railroad that led slaves out of the South. It is said by some that the room once held a constant stream of men and women seeking their way out of the South and into the relative safety of the Union states in the North.

In the chamber there were ledges that had been carved into the sides of the walls. These ledges seemed to serve no apparent purpose, although they made a great place to sit, or to store one's belongings.

The chamber had once extended much further, but the far end of the room had been blocked off. Someone had erected a tight and impassable wall of bricks, sandstone blocks and concrete.

Beyond this wall, however, was where the real mystery of the caves began.

You had only to place your ear to the cold surface of the bricks and listen to the low moan of a stale wind that was being sucked through countless passages. And

# A Guide to the Ghosts of Lincoln

standing there, far below the surface of the earth, your ear pressed against the ancient rocks, if you could quiet your beating heart, you could always hear the voices.

They were faint, and faraway, but they were voices.

The sealed-off passage must have led to the series of tunnels that wound their way throughout the area. It was through these tunnels that inmates from the Penitentiary escaped. It was through these tunnels, the legends also claimed, that patients from the State Hospital attempted their escapes.

It was behind this thick wall of bricks and concrete that you were not allowed. When you listened you could hear the voices; perhaps they were the voices of living human beings, coming from the basement of some room in the Penitentiary; but perhaps they were the echoes of voices that had spoken a century before.

In the early 1970s, Robbers' Cave was closed to the public due to the danger of cave-ins. They remained closed for a number of years until 1985 when the family who owns the property reopened them to the public. There is a modest fee charged and only a limited number of people are allowed in the cave at any one time. However, if you can brave the darkness of the underworld, it is worth your while to explore the dark mysteries of Robbers' Cave.

# The Pawnee Dance

The old man liked his trinkets. They were nothing to others, but the glass beads, silver medals and brass buttons had—it was said—a special magic, for they had been presents from the very first white men.

He fingered them every once in awhile and then carefully placed them in the leather pouch he always wore at his side. The pouch held magic: the feathers, bones and clay figures inside had provided the old man with great power in his younger days, it had protected him from the danger of battles with the Sioux and had led him to a great many buffalo.

As a boy he had listened to his Pawnee grandfathers talk of the day the white-eyes would come out of the sunrise. There was much discussion, even back then, what such stories would mean to the Pawnee.

He was still a boy when the first white men arrived, they came seeking the great water to the west. He was still a boy, but already he had gained much of his magical powers.

There were those who argued that they must kill every white they saw or otherwise there would be a plague. The boy did not believe this and raised his voice in pro

## A Guide to the Ghosts of Lincoln

test. He knew that the whites were powerful and that to fight them meant certain death for the Pawnee.

So, at first, they did not fight, but instead greeted the travelers with dances and feasts. Those early white men gave him beads and a mirror and then left. Soon, there were others. There were troubles, but his magic was strong and wherever he would be the people around him were not harmed by the white man's bullets.

This is not to say there wasn't bloodshed. Many people died in small battles—one on one—or because of simple misunderstandings. At these times the people of his band would come to him and beg him to seek revenge, to fight the whites, but he never would. "To fight them would mean our death—the death of the children and the children yet to be born," he told them.

And so, slowly, painfully, the Pawnee came to be accepted by many white settlers as "good Indians," especially when compared to the Sioux who never missed an opportunity to express their displeasure with gunfire. Because he and his band of Pawnee did not fight back, because they gave up the land that was theirs forever and because they did not stand in the whites' way, they survived.

It was in his middle years that he first began to have the dream. He slept with his leather pouch of magic trinkets near him. He slept in the long house and the tepees and out in the open prairies, but in each place the dream came to him. There was a great river, and on this river there were many boats with men who fish-ed, but no one caught anything. On one boat—it was a great wooden canoe with the head of a buffalo carved into it—a single fisherman cast out his net and drew in great schools of fish. In the dream the fish were shaped like men and they danced at the Great Fisherman's feet in the bottom of the boat.

He told his dream to his band of Pawnee and explained that it meant good times for his people. The men-fish in the boat were the Pawnee, and they would one day be protected by a great fisherman and that wonderful things would then happen.

What came instead were great battles with the whites, were countless covered wagons, were migrations that forced the Pawnee onto smaller and smaller reservations. Still, he did not waver in his belief that to fight the whites was death.

In those terrible days of bloodshed, death and long marches to new reservations his dream came to him nearly every night. Sometimes the great canoe would be surrounded by other, smaller, canoes, and sometimes it would be alone, but always it was the same: the single Fisherman's nets would be full of dancing Pawnee fish-men.

Then came the days of living on the reservation along the Loup River. While there one day a group of whites came into the village. They asked for him and were led to his tepee.

They stood in front of his tepee and read from a piece of parchment in the white tongue. Men in tall black hats

# A Guide to the Ghosts of Lincoln

and dark clothes then gave speeches and pointed at him. They slapped him on his back and shook his hand.

They gave him more trinkets, silver and blue and red and some with pictures of white men and others with pictures of the buffalo.

Finally someone who understood translated the white men's words for him. He was being thanked for his loyalty and peacefulness to the whites. They had come to give him gifts A short white man with a red nose spoke.

"They want to know what else you would like," the translator told him.

He did not have to think. "More of these," he said and held up the badges and medals.

When this was translated to the whites they all laughed.

"We will give you more of those," a white said, "but what else do you want?"

By now there was quite a crowd gathered about. The whites were all in a circle about him, but further away he could see his own people, his own grandchildren and the grandchildren of his friends, brothers and cousins.

"They want to give me more?" he asked slowly.

The translator nodded. "Whatever you want," he said.

Around him it suddenly grew silent. The whites watched him, and from a distance his people watched him, silent now too. He closed his eyes. When he opened them, he knew what to say.

# A Guide to the Ghosts of Lincoln

"I want a place where the bones of my people will be safe from the whites," he said.

The translator stared at him a long moment in silence. Then he turned and spoke to the others. For a long moment none of them spoke either, and then they gathered and talked.

The translator said: "They must talk to others." At that the white men mounted their horses and rode off as suddenly as they had come.

But he had new medals and he did not think much more about it.

But his dream of the Great Fisherman came no more. And his nights were often without sleep.

Then, just before his people were about to begin their spring dances, three white men arrived at the reservation, leading a horse. They wanted him to come with them to the town of Omaha, they had another gift. Some people warned him not to go, but he trusted the white men and mounted the horse they offered.

They took him to the town and there was a ceremony there. Men and women came to listen and watch and clap while the whites talked on and on. That day somemeone handed him a piece of paper.

"That is it," a translator explained. "That is your gift."

After some attempts the translator was able to explain to him that the white people had agreed that some Pawnee could be buried off of the reservation, in the desolate lands along the divide south of the tiny village

## A Guide to the Ghosts of Lincoln

of Lincoln. They would be able to rest there undisturbed in *perpetuity*.

It took more time, but the translator explained what this meant. For the Pawnee, *everything* was in *perpetuity*. For the Pawnee there was no past, or future, there was only the present. Only the sky and the earth lasted forever.

He took the paper and they bid him farewell. He rode alone back to the reservation.

At the reservation preparations were being made for the big feast. There was to be much dancing and singing. The people, when they learned of the paper he had received about the place south of Lincoln, were pleased.

But he was troubled. At night he was now troubled by a dark dream. He could no longer see, and no longer touch, but he could hear the roar of great beasts over his head. In his dream these beasts crawled on a rock path with great noise and smoke and would not give him peace. Then he felt a part of his rib being torn from him and taken far away. A broken wing of a bird was being dropped on his head.

The dream came again and again in his later years. He shuddered at what it could mean. His leather pouch of magic was no help, for the magic of the dream was greater. Always he dreamed it: the darkness, the voice of the crawling beasts, the smoke, and the part of him—sometimes his rib, at other times his children and grandchildren—being torn from him.

When he died he was a very old man. Even some

# A Guide to the Ghosts of Lincoln

white people came to the reservation when he died. There were dances and ceremonies to honor the dead, although even by then many of the younger Pawnee did not know how death had been treated in the old days.

He was buried on the divide in the open prairies south of Lincoln.

By his death in the late 1880s the Pawnee way of life in Nebraska was largely a thing of the past. The Pawnee reservation was disbanded and the land opened to homesteaders. There were Indian schools and places in Oklahoma where the Pawnee were being taught white man's ways, where they were being taught to farm, to cut the earth and grow hay. When he died there were even Pawnee children who did not know a single word in the Pawnee tongue. Most everyone around him did not even believe in the magic of his leather pouch.

But the pouch was buried with him, his trinkets and their magic resting beside his head in the earth.

In any event, he was to lay undisturbed in *perpetuity*, but *perpetuity* did not take into account archeological expeditions, or the march of the progress of the Twentieth Century.

His bones have been disturbed by scientists trying to find out just how the Pawnee lived. His grave his been disturbed most recently by the State of Nebraska which made the area near there a wayside area for U.S. Highway 77. It is marked as a prairie preserve, a place where the quiet and undisturbed prairie can still be experienced much as it was when the Indians roamed the

## A Guide to the Ghosts of Lincoln

area.

But the area is not quiet. Since the location was made a wayside area in the 1970s, much has happened.

It is always in the earliest hours of a new day--in that dark hour just before the dawn--that the beating of the drums, far away and muffled, can be heard. The southeast Nebraska area's most mythical ghost is restless. The sound of these drums have even been recorded on tape and many have heard them beating.

However, the vague and shadowy outline of an ancient man dressed in traditional Indian clothing has been seen at the wayside area by several people, including maintenance workers. It is common that this faint, white wisp in the darkness appears to be dancing: the knee and heel rising, then falling in a rhythmic beating.

The great feasts and dances of the Old Way have passed into history. The secrets of the primitive world of the Pawnee have now all turned to ashes and dust and are buried at the head of a peaceful man who, on the day he died, clung to his leather pouch with tears in his eyes.

# Near Twenty-second and Harrison

Contrary to popular myth, a house need not be old to have a history of hauntings. Although it appears not to stand out among the newer homes in the neighborhood, this comfortable home has its own very peculiar history.

The first family to own the home was a happy family. Neighbors can still remember a couple with a small child who kept mostly to themselves, but were generally happy and pleasant. They had moved in while the entire neighborhood still was quite new—in the late 1940s. But even then, the house was said to have its own peculiar feel about it. Even then it seemed to keep its own distance from the other houses—for it projected an atmosphere of coldness.

The young family had lived there about a year when early one morning the neighborhood was awakened by sirens in the vicinity. An ambulance pulled into the driveway. A stretcher was carried inside and a long while later, someone was removed.

The neighborhood story is that the woman had awakened early in the morning hours to find that her husband was not in bed. She got out of bed to look for him.

When she found him, he was dead. He had hanged

# A Guide to the Ghosts of Lincoln

himself with a short piece of rope from the closet of their baby daughter's bedroom.

Shortly after the funeral, the woman and her child moved away.

There were a few other owners, and then the Jespersens moved in. Matilda Jespersen remembers the ghost quite well, for she grew up in the house.

"When we were kids, we never thought much about it. We talked to the ghost and treated it as if it were a member of the family." She laughs now, remembering the spirit as one might recall an old friend.

"Things would happen all the time," she said. "We were used to it. I think it would have been worse if all of a sudden things *stopped* happening."

Matilda remembered one morning in particular. It was a school day and she had been transferred to Prescott School, after the elementary school at Irving Junior High had been discontinued.

"I was up early so that I could make it to school on time. I remember I used to think it was so far to walk to Prescott! Anyway, the rest of the family was still in bed, although I think my father was awake and shaving. I had just poured a bowl of Rice Krispies or something for breakfast when I heard someone knocking on the door to the closet downstairs." Matilda shook her head. Her long blond hair rustled against her shoulders. "That did give me a start. I mean, the knocking wasn't some little tapping; it was as if someone was pounding frantically."

# A Guide to the Ghosts of Lincoln

She sat at the kitchen table a long while without moving. In a few moments the pounding stopped.

"It didn't just stop. . .it sort of tapered off. Like he grew tired, or something."

Everyone in the Jespersen household referred to the spirit as "him." They all felt it was a masculine spirit. They always had.

"My father came down for breakfast a little while later. I couldn't decide if I should tell him about it."

Matilda had studied her father's sleepy face and had decided to wait and share her story when her mother joined them. When her mother came down a little while later, Matilda told them what she had heard.

"My mother just sat there. I think she was getting a bit weary of everything that was happening in the house. Maybe a bit frightened as well." Matilda pursed her lips and drew her tongue across them. "My father, on the other hand, first laughed, and then made some comment about the ghost getting too big for his britches. I remember that line exactly. 'The ghost is getting too big for his britches.' I wouldn't go near the closet door, but Father did. He went to open it, but the door was stuck. He pulled and pulled, but it wouldn't open."

Matilda said that when he walked away from the door, it swung open by itself. The three of them stared at the door without speaking.

The Jespersens lived in the house for nearly twenty years, raising their family. Finally, they moved; the

## A Guide to the Ghosts of Lincoln

house no longer met their needs.

There were a series of owners then, for the next eight years. Now Sally Schrader and her two children have occupied the house for the last several years.

Sally was not surprised to find the house had a long history.

"The very first night we stayed here," Sally said, "there was a tapping noise coming from above the stairs. Funny thing was, the kids weren't bothered by it at all, but boy, I was."

About a week later Sally came down the stairs in the morning and there was a coffee cup on the table. Normally there wouldn't be anything too unusual in finding a coffee cup on the table, especially in a house with two children. But this cup was from a special set of dishes that Sally kept on a high kitchen shelf, and used only on very special occasions.

At first she thought about it only a little, deciding that Kevin or Christine had taken it down. However, when she asked them about it later, she discovered that neither child had touched the cup.

Nothing unusual enough to attract her attention happened for some time. Then on the evening of the 1980 Presidential elections, Sally was watching the election returns on television.

"I sent Kevin to the store to get some milk. I was a bit chilly so I went upstairs to get a blanket off my bed. On my way up the stairs I felt something rush past me. It was so distinct that I stopped dead in my tracks."

# A Guide to the Ghosts of Lincoln

It was happening too quickly for Sally to even be scared. "The floorboards on the steps above me continued to creak just as if somebody was walking up the stairs. They continued one by one, all the way to the top of the stairs."

When Kevin returned from the store, he came up the stairs where his mother was standing. As they stood there, they both heard a door on the first floor slam shut.

"It was the door to the downstairs closet," Sally said. "There was no way it could have just swung shut, because it is always popping *open*—we usually have to block it with something to keep it closed."

There have been a few similar incidents since that November evening, but Sally can only recall two events which she classified as "major."

The first was about a year later when she and a friend were returning home from a Nebraska football game. As she was unlocking the door, they both heard a loud knocking from inside the house. The children were spending the weekend at their father's. As she opened the door, they both heard the sound of a human voice, although it seemed far, far away. It sounded as if it had said a single, one-syllable word. It was a man's voice that had said, distinctly though distantly, the word "ord" or perhaps the word "heard."

The second "major" incident was in early 1983 when Sally's youngest, Christine, complained that she felt something push past her as she stood near the bottom of the stairs. It was in the morning, just as she had come down to breakfast.

"I'm more of a believer than the kids are," Sally said. "They don't believe there is anything spiritual about the house. But then, they don't like to talk about it either."

# Bloody Mary's House

Some of the darkest spirits that roam this earth are not those of the long dead, too fond of their earthly lives to give them up, nor the wisps of past events that now repeat themselves endlessly in the dark hours of night. No. Many of the truly evil spirits on this earth are those that dwell in the souls of the living.

Bloody Mary is the creation of that dark side of human personality. She is the stepchild of rage and hatred; the daughter of our own neglect of compassion. It is we who must accept the responsibility of her existence.

Mary was born in 1871, the only child of a second-generation pioneer family. Her grandfather had come to Nebraska in 1861 and had settled on the same low ridge where Bloody Mary's house still stands. From that ridge he could look out over the wide, empty valley to the south. One day that valley would cradle the town of Lincoln.

Mary's mother died early in her life, and little is known of her father. One story, however, does survive about her earliest years.

One evening, when Mary's father had gone off to town, Mary was outside caring for her goats. A noise caused her to look up. Emerging from the small clump

# A Guide to the Ghosts of Lincoln

of trees at the creek below were three Indians.

Mary was not particularly alarmed at the sight, since the Indians would often come by their homestead to watch as she and her father worked. They never asked for it, but sometimes her father would offer them corn.

As she studied this small group of Indians something began to work in her heart. A slight edge of fear caused her to glance toward the house.

Two younger men walked on either side of an ancient one. The old man wore a much more traditional outfit than did the younger two. He carried a small pouch in his left hand.

Mary did not move. She let the tree Indians approach her. It was obvious that they wanted something, but she was not certain what it would be. It wasn't until the old man was nearly facing her that she realized he was blind. His eyes looked out and beyond her, and did not focus on the objects that were close by.

The three of them stopped, and the old man stood facing her. For a long moment nothing happened, and when he finally spoke, it was in his native language. His voice was soft, but forceful and direct.

When he had finished speaking, he opened the small pouch that he carried. He removed a handful of dust from it. He spoke again, and tossed the dust into the air above Mary's head.

Still, she did not move. The old blind Indian held her there; and she was powerless, watching the dust blow past her and toward the house.

## A Guide to the Ghosts of Lincoln

The old man reached into the pouch again. This time he removed a small bone of some kind. He waved this about Mary, and spoke again. Now the voice was that of an old man: soft, broken and sad. He waved the hand with the bone out over the long and vacant valley before them where the infant town of Lincoln stood. Then he moved it back over Mary.

Only then did she notice the other two men in any detail. Neither was well fed and their skin showed the marks of disease. Suddenly the three of them turned, and the younger men led the old man back to the trees at the creek. As they reached the cottonwoods and box elders along the slough, they released the old man and he felt along the bark of the trees to find his way. They disappeared into the trees, and in a moment Mary heard the sound of horses riding away.

When her father returned, Mary told him what had happened.

"You did the right thing," he said simply, "in not running away from them."

The tragic death of his wife had affected Mary's father. Mary was his only child and he had to rely on her for the chores that were the expected work of several sons.

He did not live long after the death of his wife. We may imagine that when her mother died, her father's spirit had broken as well, for he was a man of few words, but with a kind heart.

It was said that he lingered over his death for months

and that Mary divided her time between farm work and caring for her father.

For a while after his death, Mary was able to hold onto all of the farm by a backbreaking schedule of work and by hiring others to help as well. Finally though, she was forced to sell a portion of the farm, for it was more than she could handle by herself. She did manage to retain ten acres of the original acreage for herself. On those acres she continued to raise a bit of corn, and her favorite: a small herd of goats. She kept the ten acres the rest of her life. The ten acres and the old house.

The house had been built in anticipation of a large family. Its large porch could hold a small army, and the walls were built with the idea that additions would soon be constructed.

For the next several decades Mary lived alone in the large house. It sits a small distance off the road, just at the intersection of two country roads. Now the city of Lincoln chews at the edge of nearby fields. A wide porch and rickety steps outline the tall wooden house.

For a while Mary taught in the schools that were opening in the rapidly growing city. Often she would work on the far side of the city, and when this was the case she would rise long before dawn, and ride in her buggy to the school. But she liked her work and she liked being around children.

It was as if Mary were a born teacher. The students who were in her classrooms—now in their own silver years—can still recall her distinguished thin figure, and

# A Guide to the Ghosts of Lincoln

the stern eyes that would melt into warmth and kindness at the drop of a hat.

Mary continued to dress in her long dark skirts that were outlined in white lace, well into the 1950s. She would stand on the playground with a large whistle that dangled upon the starched ruffles of her blouse. The children would run and play under her watchful and compassionate eye.

Even when she was in her 70s and 80s, Mary occasionally would work as a substitute teacher. A person was considered useful in those days, no matter what their age. In the mid to late 50s she "retired" and returned to concentrating all of her work on her small farm.

By then much of her small ten acres was being planted and harvested by her neighbors, but Mary still kept goats. Her goats were tied to a long rope that was attached to the large elm tree in the front yard. They would lazily eat their way in a large circle about the tree, coming to the end of the line just at the edge of the fields of corn.

Mary would watch them from the rocking chair she always kept on the porch. From this vantage point she could see her favorite pets, the field, the creek and the twinkling lights of the city in the distance.

She would look out over the land that her grandfather had settled nearly a century before and beyond to the wide valley where—like a growth of its own—the city inched its way closer and closer. Now, at night, she could even hear its noises. These sounds had always

## A Guide to the Ghosts of Lincoln

before been foreign to her house and her land: sounds of movement, of automobiles. And now she would even notice the lonely lights of a car work its way up 27th Street from the city. And as she watched, she could feel a far away sense of dread.

Inside the car were three high school kids driving around having a good time. They liked to explore the edges of the city, the dark lanes where houses and unknown roads popped up like continents before them. The car radio was on, and loud. The inside of the car smelled of King's hamburgers and malted milk.

Although a faint glow remained in the west, it was night. The fading light was enough for them to trace the faint outline of an old woman who sat on the porch of an ancient farmhouse.

They pulled the car to a stop at the intersection of the two country roads. The three faces peered through the darkness. The old woman in the rocking chair stared back, barely moving in her chair.

"Boy," someone said, "look at that."

"Is that weird or what?"

"It's a lady, isn't it?"

"I think so."

Someone pointed. "What's that?"

"Where?"

"It's goats. Three goats," they shouted. "She has pet goats!"

In a moment they noticed that the house behind her was unusually dark. No light drifted from the windows.

# A Guide to the Ghosts of Lincoln

"That's because she has no electricity, dummy."

The driver said, "No electricity? That's impossible."

"Look," the other said, "do you see any electrical lines going to the house?"

Very slowly she rose up off of her rocker. She stood in the doorway a long while and stared out at the car.

"Look at her," they said from the car. "She's dressed like something out of the last century."

She disappeared into the old house.

"This is unbelievable."

Almost like prairie fire the news spread of the old woman who lived on the edge of the city without electricity and who guarded over her goats. She lived in a big old farmhouse on top of a low ridge. She never spoke, but simply rocked in her chair and watched the goats.

It was unavoidable that the story would grow and be twisted through the mill of gossip and myth. She was said to come out of her house only in the evening. She was said to be mean, chasing anyone who dared to step on her property with a stick. Some said that she took pot-shots at cars that lingered too long at the intersection. Someone said that her name was Mary.

Soon, you weren't anybody if you hadn't at least heard about Bloody Mary.

# A Guide to the Ghosts of Lincoln

### 2.

A car drove up to the intersection at Mary's house. The engine was idling; then it was still.

Inside the house Mary sat in her bed and listened. She knew the sounds of her house, for she had spent every night of her nearly ninety years here. She could tell just by the sounds that it was very early in the morning. Perhaps only 3 a.m. Mary sat in the stillness and listened. She expected that the car would drive on.

It did not. Faintly, although she could not be certain, she heard the muffled sound of a car door being shut. Then another.

Mary sat upright. If they were out of their car that meant they would be on her property. Maybe even on her porch soon. That evening she had read of an elderly woman who had been held at gunpoint in her own house.

She sat in a silence that could terrify an army. In the rafters above her she could hear the pattering of feet. That would be a small family of mice she hadn't the heart to set traps for them, for they didn't harm anything.

For a long while nothing happened. She could feel her own chest heave with her breathing, only slightly faster than normal.

*There was someone on her porch!*

The floorboards near her rocking chair, where she had

# A Guide to the Ghosts of Lincoln

walked for decades, creaked under the pressure of a weight much heavier than her own. They moaned again. A second person had crossed over them.

There was a thump against her front door and with it Mary sprang from her bed. Her breathing came quickly now, and if her heart had not raced so, she might have been surprised at the speed with which she was moving.

The gun had been her father's. He had taught her how to clean it and care for it. She had even hunted pheasant and quail with it, but for the last several years it had lain in a trunk at the foot of her bed with the other few articles of her lifetime of memories.

She had opened the trunk and felt for the big gun instinctively. She could now hear the soft sound of voices on the porch. Men's voices.

Outside the men talked in strained whispers. The whispers rose a bit with anger. One of them was about to turn back, but lingered at the edge of the porch. The other stood near a window.

"All right, coward," the one near the window hissed. "I'll do it alone."

"It's not worth it," the other shot back. "There's nothing here."

The one near the window did not answer, but turned to the glass. He clawed with a small screwdriver near the base of the pane and managed to wedge the tool beneath it. He put his weight on the screwdriver and the window slid a bit in its track, but it was not enough to get his fingers under the frame. He reset the

# A Guide to the Ghosts of Lincoln

screwdriver and pushed again.

The big gun was heavier than she had remembered. Her arms ached and strained just to lift it level. But her heart now raced as it had never done before. She wasn't afraid of death. At least she did not think so, but she wanted to have at least a fair chance against it. In the darkness she moved through the rooms of her house. In this darkness was how she had spent countless nights of her life. Through the faint glowing light of the city, she could see the figure of a man at the kitchen window. The scraping noise he was making was quite loud. Whoever it was was anxious to get in. Her trembling thumb felt along the cool metal of the big gun until it found the hammer and clicked it back.

By clawing at the glass, the man was able to wedge his fingers under the window frame. He put all of his strength into his arms, but the window would not move.

"Come on." The man at the edge of the porch stood with one leg suspended over the ground, the other on the porch, as if frozen in the night air. "Forget it."

"Coward," the one at the window said. With a great effort he was able to move the window slightly, but it was not enough for him to enter. He covered his elbow with his jacket and drove it through the pane. Glass exploded into the kitchen, and over the pantry floor.

Inside, Mary lowered the gun and fired. The shot took away most of the man's head.

## A Guide to the Ghosts of Lincoln

### 3.

Mary was never brought to trial, but after the shooting the legend of the old woman in the house grew enormously. Bloody Mary had grown into her nickname.

For the first several months after the shooting, no cars would stop at the intersection, although they paraded by endlessly radios blaring and countless round faces pressed against the glass, peering up at the old house.

In the early afternoons, if she was lucky, Mary could find a few hours to sit on her porch before another car would creep by on the road. However, her evenings of watching her goats were gone forever. In the evenings, if she dared to sit on her own porch, the cars would honk, their lights would flash and the people in the cars would yell horrible things at her. So Mary began to spend evenings inside, the lights dimmed, except for a single lantern she kept near her so that she might read a bit.

Two months after the shooting someone shot her goats. She did not hear the shots, but simply found them dead one morning, tied to the tree as she had left them the night before.

Mary was not without a few who cared for her§there were those in the city who took her side and some who even looked in on her occasionally, but when they found her body it was estimated that she had been dead at least

# A Guide to the Ghosts of Lincoln

five weeks.

The story of Bloody Mary has been told and retold countless times. And with each telling a new twist is added, a new detail is invented to mystify the life of the pioneer woman. Bloody Mary. The name alone speaks of horrors.

Her house still stands, stark and bare against the Nebraska sky. The city now has crept to the very edge of the fields her father once dreamed would be the cradle of a new beginning. The woods near the creek below the house have been cleared, and the dust of the Pawnee now provide food for stalks of tall corn. But the house still stares back at those who stop at the road. The tree where her goats were tethered still stands, spreading its ancient branches heavenward.

Naturally, there are reports of apparitions. People have seen her walking across the fields near the house. She has been seen in the windows of the house, and near the creekbed. Even the ghosts of her goats have been reported. But most often she is seen sitting on the porch in a rocking chair, staring out past the intersection of the roads to the fields beyond.

There is doubtless truth to these sightings. Even the uninformed cannot help but feel the coolness in the air if they stop a moment at the intersection and look up at the old house. A foreigner to the area can feel the presence of the house and the weight it carries.

The weight, however, is pressing down on our own shoulders. For Bloody Mary is a spirit that we, the liv-

# A Guide to the Ghosts of Lincoln

ing, have created from our own fears—a spirit we have created from our own hatred. If this small and ancient section of prairie is haunted by the spirit of Bloody Mary, we have only ourselves to blame.

# The Dorm

Like many other students at the University, Lisa Beliles does not like living in a dorm room. But unlike others, Lisa's reasons are unique.

"I live in a world of late-night hours," Lisa said. "I go to class, go out to eat, spend time at a bar or two, and then, when there is no other place to go, I go back to the dorm." Lisa tries to stay away from her room as long as possible.

"I live in the haunted room," she says with a shrug.
*The* haunted dorm room.

Lisa had a roommate. She had a series of roommates, but one by one they left the dorm when things, as Lisa puts it, "became too weird."

The legends of the haunted room go back several years at the University; and each year new twists are added to the tale of the one room, somewhere in the dorms, where the remains of a distraught student reappear.

Go back in time with those legends. Go back to the strange, electric days of the late 1960s. Walk across the campus on an early winter's day in, say, 1968.

Seasons change with the scenery, wrapping time in a tapestry, isn't that right, Mr. Jones? Lucy was in the

# A Guide to the Ghosts of Lincoln

sky with diamonds, but the girl with the sympathy for the devil lay awake in an upper level room of Pound Hall.

Lucy gets out of the bed, puts on her coat and walks out onto the campus.

Lucy writes poetry. Beautiful, sad and mystical lines which circulate about campus in the various literary magazines that are sprouting like weeds around town. In the cold air her thin, frail figure drifts like the frozen snow on a sub-zero day.

She went to Chicago that fall. Felt the heat of the times. She stood in the park and watched the police riot unfold on her generation's hopes.

Now she moves about campus—from class, to Union to class—and then back to the Union where she sits in the dark, older room which has become the area where the hippies sit. The other area, cold and modern, is for the frat rats and sorority sisters to talk about their latest dates and parties.

In the dark room there is always someone around to discuss poetry, to talk of the dark days of Nixon coming soon. And there is always someone, of course, to talk about the war.

Lucy sits blowing softly on her dark tea. On the small stage a man with a harmonica is howling out the blues. In one corner a woman sketches furiously on an art pad. In another a tall, somber man sits shuffling a pack of Tarrot cards.

She removes a small notebook from her backpack and

## A Guide to the Ghosts of Lincoln

spreads it carefully onto the table. She opens it and the thin, faint lines of her handwriting dance across its pages like tiny figures.

It is her poetry, but it is poetry which will one day gain a certain recognition. It is the same poetry others will inspect after her tragic death and claim that Lucy would have one day become famous for, had she lived. The same poetry that for a time after she has died people will read and reread.

"Your moves," she writes, "could not be matched by Billy the Kid. . ."

The room is filling with more people. A couple sit at a nearby table and discuss the Bible. She overhears them talking about how Christ drew in the sand.

A local guitar player joins the harmonica player on the stage. She recognizes him as the lead guitar player from the town's best current band: Granny's Truckstop.

She bends back over her notebook. Her words bring back the dust and heat of her childhood in the Sandhills. The words stand out on the page like the lone trees which dotted the hills.

Coyote sounds. Wind sounds. The lonesome blizzard snows of her youth.

The guitarist is swaying now, and the harmonica player slaps his hand against his leg as he plays.

Her pen scratches out words of memory and of the man she recently loved, and who she still sees occasionally. They are the phantoms she tries to put to rest with her poetry. They are some of the memories upon

## A Guide to the Ghosts of Lincoln

which her eyes can never completely close.

And then the tea is gone, the Union room is filling fast. People come in stamping their feet and covered with thick snow.

Lucy folds the notebook, stands and heads for the door. She wraps a long, woolen scarf around her neck once, twice. The end of it hangs down her back, blending with her hair.

Outside the sky has turned dark with the thick snow. Near the fountain a small group of people are holding signs and passing out literature on something. She barely notices them, walking right through their intensity with her own determined and distracted thoughts.

The white buildings sit squat and serene and tower over the surrounding parking lots and one-way streets. Each day thousands of people drive or walk past them without more than a thought. And yet these dormitories at the northeast edge of the University campus are the dwellings for thousands of students, who each year try to make the tiny rooms into some kind of a home.

Tiny cubicles of stone and plaster and sterile desks. A room planned by someone who worked late hours to come up with a design that would force the occupant into the tiny desk-top area; that would ensure that the occupant would spend what little time she spent in the cubicle studying. A couple of bookshelves, a closet, and two beds line each room, but the central attraction is the desk.

Lucy now sits at that desk. She is a very good student, an honor's student, in fact, and her copies of Faulkner and Aristotle are well worn and studied. But it is the Emily Dickinson, the Dylan Thomas and the Maria Rilke which are dog-eared and marked.

She sits at the desk and carefully places the notebook with the poetry in the center of the space. She opens to a blank page near the back and slowly tears it out so that she can hear each of the tiny holes rip apart from the wire binding.

This page she spreads out in front of her and smooths with her delicate hand as if it were the bedspread for a tiny princess.

She takes out a pen from a small coffee can of them on the desk. Her younger brother made the can for her at school, he covered the outside with felt and drew pictures of cattle and yucca: the scenes from their home in the Sandhills. Lucy has attached her own more recent mementoes to the felt: a "peace now!" and a "McCarthy" presidential button; a faded and dried flower.

The pen she has selected has a fine thin point and dark, India ink. She holds it above the paper and pauses, before she places it on the lines and writes the few words.

The police believe that she must have used the chair to break through the window. They can not understand how no one responded to the sound of the crash. It may be, they theorize, no one could get there fast enough.

Lucy's body fell the five floors onto the fresh snow

# A Guide to the Ghosts of Lincoln

of the sidewalk in front of the dorm.

At her funeral, even way out in the Sandhills, someone will be singing a Simon and Garfunkel song.

Time it was, and what a time it was, it was a time of confidences, a time of change and of time passing. And as it passed the room took on its own life.

For the rest of the term Lucy's room was left vacant. Too many curiousity seekers came by it to make it really useful for students. Suddenly, in death, this quiet, delicate and shy woman became famous on campus.

When the room was reopened the housing department had trouble finding someone to take it. Anyone who knew the story of what had happened there found reasons to keep away from it. But even after the room was filled, there were problems.

The first student who stayed there suddenly withdrew from school. Emotional problems, was the reason officials gave. Couldn't stand the stress of the University environment. Something inside of her snapped.

From then on, roommates who had been good friends fought and parted ways, perfectly healthy students moved from the room in Pound Hall with chronic headaches and hallucinations.

Lucy started to return.

In the dark night she began to appear standing over her old bed. Residents awoke to screams. To the sound of breaking glass. To books crashing from the desk onto the floor.

Lisa Beliles turned down her Walkman. Bon Jovi was

her favorite. She liked the way you can dance to them.

"I guess I am a little strange myself," she said. "I like the room. No one else ever wants to be my roommate, and I am used to that."

Lisa admits that the room "weirds her out." "I don't mind the things that happen... I just can't stay there *all* the time. It would drive me crazy."

Lisa says she doesn't mind waking in the middle of the night out of a deep and restful sleep to realize that the dorm is perfectly still, unearthly quiet. She knows what to expect next. She glances around and then she sees it.

"It is kind of a haze... as if it was a cloud of smoke, only it is her. I mean, it is in the shape of this woman. No face, or anything, but you can tell it is a woman, a thin, short woman."

Lisa simply watches the shape. "I kind of stare her down." Eventually it fades, growing lighter and lighter until it simply disappears.

"If I let it, I would get the creeps," she says.

Lisa did not know the entire history of the room, and did not know Lucy's name. Now, she says, she understands why so much has been happening to her.

"I not only see her, but sometimes I swear I can hear someone else at the desk when I am sitting there." The faint sound of paper being rustled floats on the air during late nights of studying.

Lisa understands now why she sees Lucy's shape so often, why her own books are always misplaced, or sud-

# A Guide to the Ghosts of Lincoln

denly fall off the bookshelf without notice.

Lisa turns down the tape. "I write poetry," she says, "people say I am pretty good."

# The State Capitol Building

The ride to the top floor of the state capitol building is slow by modern-day standards. The old elevators, only recently made independent from needing a human operator, creak and whir and rise up the 13 floors to the observation level. Ears popping, and slightly dizzy, every week thousands of tourists step out of the small cubicles and onto the stone floor of the observation level.

The view from high above the city is what everyone wants to see. They look out over the city checking roof tops and street corners, looking for their own homes. They comment on how the city seems to have grown so quickly, how it was only yesterday when there was nothing but cornfields where now there are nothing but more houses. They talk, these tourists, they talk and point and look out while children run and scream around the circumference of the building. If there is silence it is filled with the faint echo of the traffic far below. If there is silence it is filled with the sound of the wind whistling through the ornate stone work which towers above the observation level another three stories to the dome and the huge statue of the sower.

But in the quiet, the sensitive ones hear another sound.

## A Guide to the Ghosts of Lincoln

They are those who have told of hearing the deep and mournful sounds of a man crying. His sobs are far off, and distant; but those who have heard them say they are there and that if you stand on the southeast side of the building and listen, and if it is the right time, you will hear them too.

There is more than a little evidence which suggests that the crying these people hear is more than the wind, or the cooing of mourning doves.

Years ago during the Christmas season, the capitol dome would be strung with a brilliant cape of bright lights. The tradition lit up the hearts of many of the city's residents, but it provided something more akin to fear in a lesser appreciated segment of society.

Who would be fool enough to climb out on the dome to string the lights?

To reach the dome a staircase winds around the inner walls of the observation level's rotunda. Stand in the rotunda and look up at the glass windows and you will see the shadow of the staircase, squeezed between this glass and the outside windows. The staircase was built into this interior space so that it would be invisible from the outside, and difficult to see from the inside.

These hidden stairs lead up and around the rotunda until they reach a small, rusted and bolted door. Only rarely is this door unlatched and opened, but when it is it opens directly under the statue of the sower. When it is flung open there is nothing but the smooth and sloping surface of the capitol's dome between the tiny door-

## A Guide to the Ghosts of Lincoln

way and a 17 story drop to the ground.

To string the canopy of Christmas lights a worker had to venture out on the dome, attach them and then spread them evenly over the entire surface of the golden dome. It was like being spread-eagle on the surface of a gigantic slippery egg, suspended high above the earth.

A harness would be rigged up and a man would climb up the steps, open the hatch and feel the hammer-blow of the winter wind on his face. He would try to ignore the floating sensation in his stomach and, after testing the strength of the his harness and saftey ropes one last time, he would crawl slowly out onto the surface of the dome.

It was not a job many men volunteered to do, no matter how great their Christmas spirit might have been. That is why, for a long while, inmates from the state penitentiary volunteered to take the risk of such a job. In exchange for their efforts they received the thanks of the state, the city and, to be sure, a certain bit of recognition the next time the parole board met.

Still, to be lowered out onto that curve toward death must have been worth much more.

It must have been worth much more to a man who, in 1967 or '68, was selected to perform the ritual. One evening after the building was closed for the day, a guard from the penitentiary accompanied him up the elevators and to the bottom of the staircase in the observation level's rotunda. From there a couple of maintenance workers climbed up the staircase with the inmate, ex-

# A Guide to the Ghosts of Lincoln

plaining how the safety harness worked.

Already the air was cold and thin. They reached the top of the stairs and the small rusted door. The workers attached the ropes, working amid the clutter of the strings of Christmas lights. Finally, with a last check of the man's harness, the latch was turned and the trap door flung open.

Slowly, he was lowered out of the door, feet first and stretched out on his belly. The workers started to feed him the long strings of lights.

All went fine at first. He slowly moved across the dome, spreading the lights and the net of wires as he moved. The net nearly covered a quarter of the dome.

This convict, after seasons of being held in the tight captivity of his tiny cell, now had the open and boundless air on every side.

They say that the fear is much worse than the fall. The fear creeps into your body from the feet up and a weakness comes. It hits the stomach first, and then the blood leaves your head. Even a dream, the imagining of such a fall, wakes us up from the deepest sleep with a jerk.

No one, perhaps not even the man himself, knows for sure exactly what happened, but at some point, stretched out on the thin rope above the darkening city, with no footholds, and only thin cracks on the surface of the dome in which to squeeze his fingers, the convict panicked.

His muscles tightened. The blood rushed from his

## A Guide to the Ghosts of Lincoln

head and arms, and yet the vessels in his temples pounded his life's blood until they burst.

Far below the houses began to twinkle with the festive lights of the season. High above, on the open surface of the capitol dome, a man's endless scream cut through the cold Nebraska winter's night. It echoed and reverberated through the air and through the years since then for those who listen for it in the rushing wind on top of Nebraska's most famous building.

Another theory for the strange sights and sounds some have witnessed on top of the building is connected to the seldom used spiral staircase which leads up the entire length of the building and reaches the observation level in the southeast corner of the floor.

A large wire gate has been added at the top of the staircase. The gate is often locked, closing it off from the public, and for good reason. The spiral staircase has no central support, but is attached on the outside to the walls, so that when you lean over the railing and look down the center of the stairwell it is an open drop to the bottom, a dozen floors below.

The great building had been plagued for years by children who dropped coins down this stairwell, unknowingly denting the hand rail and walls.

But the children's coins aren't the reason for the gate which isolates this staircase. In the late 1950s a man leaned too far over the edge of it in order to peer down the spiral. He leaned too far, grew dizzy, lost his balance and bounced and crashed ten floors to his death. There

# A Guide to the Ghosts of Lincoln

was a rumor that he was distraught over the fact that his best friend married his girlfriend. It may be the remnants of his anguished cries and screams which reverberate today in the tall ceilings of the building.

The capitol building is apparently full of spirits. Below the bottom floor of the building is the true basement. This cavernous space is dark and damp and in places one can still see the outlines of the foundation of the first capitol building which stood at the same place before the current building was constructed.

In this lost netherland in the bowels of the earth, with the tall weight of the building on top of you, a certain spirit resides. It is said that all truly holy places of mankind have been holy places for ever. It is said that long before the town of Lincoln was ever founded, the Indians treated the small hill where the capitol building now stands as a holy place.

Now in the lowest basement of the building, walking down the corridors through the maze of dark hallways and tunnels, each step brings you closer to the feeling that at any moment you will come face to face with someone, or with something. Around each new corner the feeling grows more distinct. There is someone, or something here.

The silence, and the always empty hallways, brings on the fear, and the knowledge that here, deep under the building, more of the capitol's unknown residents dwell in their silent terror.

# Famous Paintings

David Schrader looked about him as if his very words might cause a haunting to occur at that precise moment. "Most everything happened in the basement," David said. "There were things that happened elsewhere in the house, but the basement was the haunted place."

The house where David lived for a number of years is one of the more famous of Lincoln's haunted houses. The sightings and apparitions that have happened in this house have been documented by several world-famous ghost hunters and psychics. It has been included in books and national publications.

David lived in the house with a few other people after a family who had lived there left. The family had been described in a book on ghosts as having had a series of unusual experiences. After the book was published, David claimed, the events in the house increased, and the mother of the family began to feel threatened by the house.

Although David lived in the house for quite some time, he never was relaxed enough to sleep well at night. He has now moved away from Lincoln. He now lives in Boston and during the days he punches information in-

## A Guide to the Ghosts of Lincoln

to a computer, so that at night he is free to play bass guitar in rock 'n' roll bands.

He would like to visit Lincoln again, and maybe even stop by the house. "But sometime in the future," he said, "and not for a while yet."

He did not know about the house's fame until he was nearly ready to move out. By then the house had already gained a certain kind of fame in his mind.

David recalled that the first day he moved into the house he had an odd "feeling". He described the feeling as if someone had just been in the house before he entered it. The events themselves began that very first night he spent in the house.

"I went to sleep in the bedroom on the first floor," David said. "I was asleep for a while and then, suddenly, I was wide awake. Now, I'm the type of guy who. . .well, first of all it takes an explosion to wake me up, and then it takes another six or seven hours before I'm fully awake." But sometime in the middle of that first night he woke up and was fully alert. It was as if it were the middle of the day.

What might have awakened him was the odd smell that filled his bedroom. It was a foul smell, and even though David could vividly remember it two years after he had left the house, he was hard pressed to describe it.

"It didn't smell like anything I have ever smelled before. Not like anything rotting, or spoiled, nor any organic smell. And yet it wasn't a chemical smell either."

# A Guide to the Ghosts of Lincoln

Other occupants of the house described a pungent odor that drifted through the rooms of the house shortly before a flurry of activity occurred.

It was some time before he was able to fall back asleep. He was not yet aware of anything too unusual about the house. Just being awakened from a deep sleep, and the strange smell in his room. Nothing else, except for the vague feeling he felt while moving in, caused him to speculate about the origins of the mystery of that house.

In the time he was awake that night he lay in the dark, listening to the silence of the house. Twice he felt a vague, but not threatening feeling that someone was nearby, but dismissed these feelings as the hallucinations one experiences on the edge of sleep.

"Just before I fell back to sleep I heard a thump," he said. "It wasn't particularly loud, or even distinct, but it did bring me fully awake again. I was a bit afraid now, though, because I thought that maybe someone had broken into the house. I didn't move for awhile, straining to hear any other noise. Nothing else happened that night and I fell asleep."

The house is an older home, but not unusually so for the northside neighborhood where it is located. From the outside one might notice only that there is a kind of darkness that seems to shroud the house, as if it sits in a shadow of its own making. The neighborhood houses are not much different, although they lack the imposing shadows of David's house.

# A Guide to the Ghosts of Lincoln

For several weeks nothing out of the ordinary happened that would remain in David's memory. However, slowly he became aware of a phenomenon he at first tried to ignore.

Initially he chalked up the misplaced objects to his ability to forget the simplest of things. David had been known to search for hours for a set of car keys that were in his pocket. There was the possibility, too, that his roommates had moved things. A coffee cup disappeared and days later was found on a ledge in the staircase that led to the basement. A gas bill would show up in the medicine cabinet of the bathroom. A box of guitar picks couldn't be found, and then was discovered in the refrigerator.

"The refrigerator," David repeated. "Now I know everyone will think I'm making this up, but after looking for them all over, they were in the refrigerator! Right in front."

Other things were moved about the house. Once a tennis shoe of one of David's roommates could not be found. Weeks later, after everyone had given up looking for it, it "appeared" in the middle of the floor of the basement.

The basement of the house is not unlike many basements in Lincoln. Built originally to provide a place for a coal bin and a coal burning furnace, the concrete walls and floor now provide a home for a wide assortment of items. Lawn chairs and unused clothing, tools and shelves of dusty magazines and books.

# A Guide to the Ghosts of Lincoln

The door to the basement was at the back of the kitchen and steep steps led down to the damp and poorly lighted basement.

One morning David stood at the bottom of the steps. He had gone down into the basement to look for a book he had used in high school. The book, he recalled, was *Miss Lonelyhearts.*

"That basement had always been a weird place because of all the drawings and pictures on the walls," David said. "Most of them were pretty straightforward kid drawings. Faces and things. I think there was a drawing of a horse. . .but they were all eerie. Like I say, I was always spooked in that basement."

One far wall of the basement was cluttered with drawings. Most of them were placed there years ago by the daughter of a previous tenant. It is said that this young girl was especially receptive to visitations by the apparitions in the house. She is claimed to have seen a spirit almost constantly in the house, and especially in the basement. Most of the time she lived in the house she came to the basement to draw on the walls. Her drawings were still there at last report, all surrounding the relief sculpture of the mysterious baby.

"That baby's face is something else," David said. "The first time I saw it I knew it was special. It wasn't like the drawings. That baby's face was. . .well, real."

No one is certain how the image of a human baby came to be set in relief in the basement wall of a house north of O Street in Lincoln, Nebraska. The face was

# A Guide to the Ghosts of Lincoln

sculpted into the wall, obviously a work of great loving care. One theory advanced for the relief is that someone who lived in the house in the 1930s carved the image to commemorate the birth of their first child, a daughter who—it is said—died in the house on her third birthday.

"I had been standing at the bottom of the steps sort of staring off at the wall with all the paintings," David said. "All of a sudden a motion caught my eye."

He had turned to face the bookshelf against another wall. He watched as one of the books actually slid across the shelf and fell onto the floor.

"I about jumped out of my skin, but I went over and inspected the shelf. The shelf was perfectly level, and the book had been placed on a pile of books that nobody had touched in months.

"I turned back toward the steps and saw a man standing near the wall. Afterwards I remembered that he didn't look at me. He was just standing there. He seemed kind of faded."

David did not wait for introductions. Assuming the figure to be that of a burglar, David spun around to find a tool to use to protect himself.

"I was shocked. I hadn't heard anyone on the stairs, and I had never seen the guy before. I figured he must be there hiding out to rob the place. I grabbed a hammer or something, and when I turned again. . .no more than half a second later. . .he had vanished."

David bounded up the steps and threw his shoulder

against the basement door. It had always stuck a bit, but now it would not budge. He bounced off the jammed door and nearly stumbled back down the dimly lit stairs.

"I wasn't in a panic or anything like that," David went on. "It really hadn't dawned on me yet that I had seen a ghost. It was simply that I had seen a strange man in my own basement and that he had disappeared. I wanted to get out of the basement so that I could call the cops, or find something to defend myself with, or something."

He continued to pound against the door. After several tries it seemed to open with ease, and he rushed out of the basement. He went straight to the phone and called the police to report a prowler in his basement.

Only after he had hung up did David begin to realize how strange the sight of the man had been. Although he had a definite shape, David was dimly aware that he had been able to see the wall behind the man, right through his torso. Also, the man had not spoken, although David himself had let out an audible gasp. And the man did not seem to notice David.

When the police arrived they searched the basement and asked David questions. Their businesslike manner only underscored how odd he felt telling them his story. He realized how silly the story must have sounded to them. He answered their questions about the man's identification. The man he had seen, David told the police, was an older man. His hair was long and dirty and he had a beard. Beyond that David could not be sure; he could not remember, for example, what the man had been wearing. He thought possibly he had been in some kind of work clothes, but he was not sure.

"I think those cops must have thought I was a looney. They poked around the house, trying to assure me that everything was all right."

Police are used to answering calls from people who hear or see people in their houses. Frightened people call the police convinced that there are strangers in their house. It is rare, however, that the police ever find someone, since most of the calls come from overactive imaginations, creating a criminal out of the wind against a screen.

"The difference was," David said, "I *knew* I had seen somebody."

About a week after this incident, a neighbor stopped David on the street and the conversation eventually led around to the police car the neighbor had noticed a few nights back. David had already grown wary of telling his "ghost" story, for he was tired of being laughed at. To his surprise, however, the neighbor brought it up.

"He came right out and asked if I had seen the man in the basement. I nearly jumped out of my skin!"

There had been a history of visits by the police to that house, the neighbor told him, and all for the same reason. A strange man had been sighted in the basement. The police were called. The man disappeared. Just disappeared.

The neighbor then let the conversation drift to the

weather and other topics, but David could not keep the lump out of his throat.

He then began to ask carefully—testing the waters for possible ridicule—other neighbors about the house. From them he learned a bit of the house's history. Someone showed him a copy of a book about ghosts. A psychic who had once visited the house on North 29th Street claimed there was not just one spirit in the house but at least three, possibly more.

He eventually learned how a man had once been murdered in the basement of the house. He had been stabbed several times in the heart with a knife. He heard the story of the baby who died in her third year.

"I searched the official records after that," David said. "But I could never find any evidence—officially anyway—of a murder in the house. However, the people in the neighborhood claimed it had happened quite a while ago, possibly as early as 1892."

There were reports of other residents of the house seeing moving lights in a small upstairs room. David had heard the stories, but for a long while he did not see the lights.

Then one night he was in the room.

"I was practicing my guitar. The curtains were drawn and there was no traffic on Fair Street outside. The door to the room was open. I looked up from my guitar and there was a light moving about the room as if someone were moving a flashlight. No, not a flashlight, really, just a light. And all of a sudden everything was deathly quiet. I remember the quiet."

The light that he saw was diffused and unfocused. It moved about the tiny room in no apparent pattern. He put his guitar on the floor and stood up, and as he did he caught the faint smell he had first noticed nearly two years before on the first night he had spent in the house. After a moment the lights and the smell faded. A bus or a truck drove by on the street below.

In recent years, other people have lived in the house. Students from the University, small families and others. Most current area residents are not comfortable talking about the house. After all, the house has become a kind of celebrity. One area resident explained that talking about such experiences only encourages whatever evils might dwell in the house to continue their activities. Others simply refused to say anything.

Nothing indicates that the events in the house have ceased and it appears to be one of the most active areas in the Midwest. Just ask David Schrader.

"If there is anything like a haunted house," he said, "that's the place."

# The Strange Disappearance of Charles M. Danca

In the very early hours of what would be a bright and cheery morning of May 16, 1917, Charles M. Danca, an up and coming Lincoln businessman rose from his bed and vanished into thin air.

Danca's roots have been traced to Germany where he was born and lived until he was about 14 years old. He then immigrated to Chicago where he lived with his uncle, a shoemaker and tanner.

After a few years, when the young Danca was old enough to try a hand at his own life, he migrated west. He came to Lincoln via the old Nebraska City Cut-Off road which ran from Nebraska City to the Platte near Grand Island.

The relative prosperity of the still new and growing community attracted him, and he decided to stay. He worked for a time in various stores along "O" Street, learning what made a good business in the town, and what made customers return to one store time and time again.

Before long, Danca had saved enough money, or had

# A Guide to the Ghosts of Lincoln

found enough investors, that he was able to purchase a small general merchandise store near downtown.

Danca's store was located near the northwest corner of the intersection of 11th and "N." His reputation as a fair and honest businessman soon brought him a steady stream of customers.

After establishing the business, and working for a number of years at it, Danca returned to Germany for a visit.

While in Germany he was to meet and marry a woman who would become the nemesis of his life. Beautiful, graceful, and with a hint of royalty, Johanna Wacholder felt she was destined to a life different than others. She was swept up by this bold and energetic young man from Lincoln and the dream of the life of a baroness in the new world excited her. Soon after their marriage, they returned to Nebraska.

It might be hard for a resident of Nebraska to believe, but Johanna was devastated when she arrived in Lincoln. The dusty, busy village surrounded by deep green and treeless fields of corn and wheat was as far from her dreams of a royal life as she could have imagined.

Danca was crestfallen and was determined to do whatever he could to make her life in the city as pleasant as he could.

"If Johanna wants it," he told his friends, "I will see to it that she gets it."

Plainly, the small single level clapboard home he had rented near 3rd and E streets would not do for Johanna.

## A Guide to the Ghosts of Lincoln

Danca soon hired contractors and architects and builders and together they began to build a house that would closer suit Johanna. First, it had to be two levels, and two levels with several rooms. It had to have a curved porch, a balcony and plenty of room for a garden. A flower garden.

Next, it had to be in a better area of town, and one where she would be able to socialize with those who mattered. Danca's house took shape in the 1700 block of E street, up several blocks, and a few social clubs from 3rd street.

Less than a year after they moved in a child was born to the Dancas. The small baby girl was their pride and joy, and often the little one cold be found crawling amid the bolts of calico or lace around the shelves of the store.

It wasn't long after that a second child was born, this one a son. The family of four was increased by a maid and a nurse for the children, who lived in the big house. The Danca store continued to prosper, although the panic of the late 1800s had closed several other businesses in the city. Still, in spite of their prosperity and their social status, Johanna was not happy. She always longed to be someone else, someone she belived she might have become if she had stayed in Germany and never ever heard of Lincoln, Nebraska.

It never comes announced, and it never misses a single soul on this earth. So it was that tradgedy struck the Danca's swiftly and without warning. One day their first born became ill with a fever. By evening the child was delirious, and in the darkest hour of the night, the joy of their life passed on to some other shore.

Danca was devastated and, as was his style, devoted himself with even greater resolve, to his business. He would leave the house before dawn and stay at the store until long after dark.

Johanna, however, took the death in a different way. She seemed to grow even more extroverted and carefree than she had ever been before. There was more than a little small talk about her around the town.

To ease her grief, and perhaps because of the talk around town, shortly after the child's death Johanna packed up and took the Danca boy on a voyage back to Germany. They would visit the homeland, she would rejuvenate her soul and perhaps even realize a bit of the tarnish that must now have appeared on her one-time dream of glory.

But fate is nothing if not unpredictable, and on the voyage her only son took ill and died in a fit of tossing and turning on board the steamer in the middle of the Atlantic.

Johanna continued on. When the boat docked she wired the news to her husband far away on the edge of the world's frontier. Instead of turning around to rejoin him, she headed for Germany.

The news of Danca's son's death filtered through Lincoln in a growing wave of gossip and sympathy, much like the same kind of news even today might still travel from friend to friend. Danca sealed himself in a cloud

## A Guide to the Ghosts of Lincoln

of grief and labor. It was an accepted fact that one did not speak to him of these tragedies if one did not wish to invite the blackest and darkest of stares.

But Danca continued his life, difficult though it must have been. He must have waited painfully for a word back from his distant wife.

Johanna dove into her old life in Germany with complete abandon. The time came for her return trip to the States and it passed without her leaving. Months came and went. Still, she remained in her old homeland, dining and dancing and entertaining. Her wealth and the mystery of a woman who had actually seen American Indians and buffalo, gave her the kind of status and special treatment for which she had always longed.

While in Germany, perhaps at one of the many social functions for which she was in constant demand, she met a man, fell in love, and despite the fact that she had a husband in Lincoln, Nebraska, married him.

The man, a baron, knew of Danca and knew that his wife was, by most standards of the law of those days, not legally his. But that did not seem to be the least concern of either Johanna or the Baron. In fact, they soon left Germany and at Johanna's insistence, set sail for the United States.

The couple settled in Denver. On their way west they passed through Lincoln in the middle of the night. They looked out the thin glass windows at the growing town where somewhere, unaware that she had returned, Johanna's first husband slept and dreamt his fitful

## A Guide to the Ghosts of Lincoln

dreams.

In Denver Johanna, with the help of the Baron's money, opened a business which today we might have called a beauty parlor. At the turn of the century, however, and because Johanna never did anything halfway, this parlor had everything. There were steam baths, young oriental girls to give massages, mud baths with the finest green clay imported from France, and even a house hypnotist who, for an additional fee, would mesmerize the client in order to restore health and beauty.

As odd as it might sound today, such a business did florish in Denver and other towns through out the west. Johanna became the talk of Denver, and unlike Lincoln, where her first husband's work had been what had gained the attention of the town, in Denver it was Johanna's business which had made her known.

Word filtered down to Danca back in Lincoln that his wife had married another man and that they were in Denver. People that knew him well watched and waited for some reaction. Many of his close friends urged him to seek damages, to take the woman to court for what she had done to him.

Danca shrugged. It was as it had always been. If it was what Johanna wanted, it was still what he tried to give her. If she wanted to live with someone else, to never see him again, well then, that was just what Danca's love for her would provide.

In the meantime Johanna's business was booming so

## A Guide to the Ghosts of Lincoln

that she and the Baron decided that they could expand their particular formula for health and beauty to other locations in the country. They considered Chicago and New York, but finally decided that San Francisco would be the location of the first expansion. The Baron was to go west and start up the business, while Johanna located managers for the Denver one. As soon as the new branch was underway in California, she would join him there and they could retire and sit back and watch their two operations make money for them.

But it was not to be. Johanna had agreed that the Baron needed help in setting up the new operation and he left Denver with a few employees from the business, including a young oriental women who gave the massages and for whom he had a considerable attraction.

Once in San Francisco he used the power of attorney that Johanna had given him to transfer the entire ownership of the business to himself. He even took the name "Johanna's Salon" for the new business and he and his new girlfriend took over all the assets.

Destitute and soon penniless Johanna finally contacted Charles Danca for help. He sent her money, against the advice of everyone, in the hopes that she might return to him.

She remained in Denver and used his money to clothe herself in as elegant dresses as she could. She wore them from tavern to tavern where she spent the remainder of Danca's love money on alcohol.

In spite of his considerable personal misfortune, Dan-

# A Guide to the Ghosts of Lincoln

ca's store and his reputation continued to grow with Lincoln. His sad story followed him around and newcomers to the town soon learned of the kindly and civic-minded citizen who carried the scars of a life that had crashed about him years before.

Through it all Danca remained in the large house which he had built for Johanna. He even retained the services of a maid who lived in the cottage above the garage and who cooked, cleaned and kept house for the solitary man.

Danca did keep a dog. A gentle and handsome German shepherd roamed the grounds of the house and slept near his master's feet each night.

In the mornings the maid would come into the house, start up the stove and fix breakfast. The dog would often wander down the stairs and scratch lightly at the door to be let out. Shortly after, often before the sun rose, Danca himself would come down the steps, walking lightly on the carpeted stairs.

One evening, on May 15, 1917, Charles M. Danca had dinner at the house with one of his closer friends, a gentleman by the name of Campbell whose own downtown mercantile business was outdoing Danca's now faltering one. In spite of this conflict, the two men were fast and close friends. The maid prepared a dinner and could hear the two of them talking and laughing over cigars and brandy after the dinner. Later she would recall how she thought that it was the happiest she had heard her boss in a long while.

She went to bed after Campbell left and some of the dishes were collected. She had heard her master go up the stairs and watched as the dog trotted up the stairs behind him. She listened as he put himself to bed. She worked a little while longer and then went out to her room to sleep.

She slept soundly and in the morning, before daylight, returned to the house, as she had done for years, to start to prepare breakfast.

As she was cooking the food she heard the dog in Danca's room barking furiously. She was concerned, but did not go up to investigate until the dog had continued to bark for some time. She climbed the stairs and went to his room. She knocked, and then, when there was no answer, she flung open the door.

The dog had been barking at the empty bed, but now that she had arrived, the dog hesitated, then bolted from his position at the foot of the bed and ran from the room.

Danca was nowhere to be found. She discovered that his glasses were still on the shelf, and since he was as blind as a bat without them, she knew he couldn't have gone far. In addition his walking stick, his billfold and his topcoat were untouched. Still, it was a mystery where he could have gone. Especially since she would have seen him had he come down the stairs.

When he did not appear for several hours the maid contacted the police. A complete search of the area was made. Word went out to be on the lookout for him. But the day passed and he did not appear at the store, or reappear at home.

Charles M. Danca was never heard from again. No one has ever come up with a plausible explanation for his sudden and complete disappearance into the thin air of a spring morning.

# Just Go East On "O"

Jake Osborn looked down over his long nose at the two young men who stood awkwardly at his front door. He dangled the key to the old house out at them. "Good place for a summer crew to live in," he said. "Probably needs a little cleaning up, but. . .well, you look it over."

Jack took the key. "Thanks," he said.

Jake Osborn went on. "Last folks to live there was a family. They left there last spring. Had them a couple of young kids, well, one day they just disappeared." Jake Osborn shook his head. He had not seen anything like it.

"Just disappeared. They still had some rent money coming to them, but they left without even asking for it."

Jack and Bill waved at Jake Osborn and drove away from the old farmer's house in the carry-all van. They were in good spirits, for the Boss had sent the two of them out from town to inspect the house where the archeological field crew would be spending the summer. It was a cool, but sunny day in late May and it was a good time to be alive.

The Boss wanted to know if the house would be adequate for the entire crew. Jack drove the state van over

## A Guide to the Ghosts of Lincoln

the graveled roads, dropped it down a gear and felt the rear wheels fishtail on the loose rocks. The location was good enough. The house stood only a mile and a half from the Indian mounds the crew would investigate on their dig that summer.

Bill leaned forward to the radio and turned up the sound. "I like this song," he said.

In a moment Jack turned it back down. "Is this it?"

Set back from the road, and sheltered by a field of unmowed grass and brambles, was a tall and thin house that seemed to glow from the dark trees that nearly surrounded it. It was built entirely from ancient limestone blocks, slightly yellowed and worn from countless seasons in the plains of eastern Nebraska. Later a man from the Nebraska State Historical Society would estimate that the house was well over a hundred years old and perhaps the oldest limestone structure in the county.

"I bet there are spiders in there," Bill said. Jack pulled the carry-all van into the yard. Bill said, "Let's tell the Boss everything was O.K. Let's go get some coffee."

Jack ignored him and parked the van near the back door. They got out of the van. A screen door hung at a slight angle against its hinges, balanced so that a slight breeze would cause it to swing back and forth. Jack fitted the key into the lock on the back door and twisted it. It opened without effort.

The door opened into a kitchen. On a table in the middle of the room was a bowl, several plates and some silverware. In the bowl were the blackened remains of a half-eaten breakfast of cereal. A spoon was practically welded to the bowl.

"Somebody left without finishing their breakfast," Jack said.

"I'm not touching that mess," Bill said. "I'll quit first."

The other rooms were in disarray. Newspapers were scattered about and personal belongings still remained in most of the rooms. A shoe here, a half-used tube of toothpaste there.

The two young men moved about the old farmhouse trying to pick up a bit of the mess, and judging whether the house would be adequate for the summer field crew. Aside from the kitchen, there were a bathroom and two other small rooms downstairs. A narrow staircase led to two small rooms connected by a single doorway on the second floor.

The upstairs was not nearly as disorderly. In fact, it appeared as if it had not even been used by the last residents. The two of them went back to the main floor. They found a doorway and opened it. A cool and stale air sprang back at them from the basement below. Both of them hesitated. There was no electricity in the house and the steep steps and dark chasm yawned up at them.

"You go right ahead," Bill said. "I'll wait up here to see if you come back alive."

"He told us specifically to check the basement," Jack said, not too convincingly.

# A Guide to the Ghosts of Lincoln

Bill eyed the narrow steps that led to the dungeon below. "Well, we could tell him that something was down there and wouldn't let us in."

Jack hesitated. Finally he turned away from the door. "All right," he said. "We'll tell him something. All I know is that I don't want to go down there."

A week later they returned in the carry-all van, filled with the work crew for the summer excavations. There were nine in the crew, including the Boss' wife, who was to serve as the cook.

It was a busy day. A moving van arrived with the larger equipment. Everything had to be unloaded and carried into the house. Two refrigerators, kitchen supplies, personal belongings. The only running water inside the house was in the kitchen. But it had to be hooked up to the windmill out in a field. A series of garden hoses was connected. The small indoor bathroom would not be used, so outhouses had to be dug and an indoor shower constructed.

It was a long, tiring day, but the crew seemed to work well together, joking and laughing as they went about their chores. In the evening most of the crew climbed up the narrow steps to the two small upstairs rooms. Most of the bunks were there, and the crew wasted no time in climbing into bed.

Everyone, except for the Boss and his wife who had a small trailer parked outside, heard the noises that first night. From inside the walls of the house and from the narrow staircase to the first floor came knocking, scrapes

# A Guide to the Ghosts of Lincoln

and once a rapid three bumps followed by a soft patting sound. In their exhaustion from the busy day, no one paid them much mind.

Jack's body ached in the morning, but after a huge and piping hot breakfast he felt better. Most of them were quiet at breakfast, but Bill chattered constantly.

"I love the outdoor life," Bill said. "Just smell that fresh air."

Everyone could tell that Bill's early morning manners might grow a bit thin in the coming months.

"What were those strange sounds?" Bill asked. "Did anyone hear those noises last night?" A few of them nodded. "Strange," Bill said.

After the crew arrived at the work site, the Boss realized that he had forgotten a compass and sent Jack in the carry-all back to the house to get it.

The Boss' wife was standing at the kitchen sink washing the breakfast dishes as Jack went through the back door. She looked at him. "So you decided to come back for the rest of the crew, eh?" she said.

"The rest of the crew?" Jack said.

"Why yes." She smiled. "Whoever you left upstairs moving the furniture around."

"There's no one upstairs," Jack said. "Everyone went with us."

Her smile faded. "Then who's upstairs?"

Jack bounded up the narrow stairs. The rooms were as he had left them, and they were empty.

The events in the following weeks were such that some

# A Guide to the Ghosts of Lincoln

explanation had to be found. The light in the main room began to fade and glow. The sounds in the night became more and more like footsteps, and they began to occur at any hour of the day or night. Objects disappeared.

At first these events were taken as a kind of joke. Peacock, though, wasn't laughing. He claimed to know something about ghosts, and he took everything a bit more seriously than the others. Almost from the start he told everyone that all indications were that they were in the presence of a powerful spirit.

Perhaps it was their first mistake, but the crew soon nicknamed Peacock's ghost. Now, when plates crashed to the floor, or the footsteps were heard, someone would simply call out, "Cut it out Clem. . .we're trying to get some sleep." What no one expected was that directing comments to the spirit worked. The footsteps would suddenly cease.

One night most of the crew were sitting around the large wooden table where they ate and played cards. "One thing ghosts like to do," Peacock began, "is to make faucets sound like there's water coming out when there isn't any. . . ." The words had barely left his mouth when, from the small and unused bathroom, the pipes began to rattle and then the sound of running water came from the sink.

The entire crew jumped up from the table and rushed into the tiny bathroom. For a long moment no one spoke. They stood speechless, staring at the gurgling faucet. After a bit, the sound faded.

# A Guide to the Ghosts of Lincoln

"Oh my god," Bill said softly.

That was the night Scott moved outside. Scott was a very devout and religious member of the crew. He took his bunk and his sleeping roll and moved them permanently outside. In another day Peacock joined him and they set up a large canvas tent. Both of them refused to have anything to do with the house, except as a place to eat their meals. What was more, their move seemed to divide the crew, and kept everyone nervous.

Events rained down now on the jittery group. One night there was a particularly heated debate. The debate centered around the question of the possible existence of ghosts. Could there be such things as ghosts?

"Even if there are ghosts," Jack was saying, "it's just possible that everything that has happened in this house is just happenstance. Just natural phenomenon."

Most of the crew, including Peacock, were sitting at the big table. The Boss and his wife were in their trailer, and Scott had hurried out to his tent as soon as dinner was finished.

Peacock shook his head. "No way," he said. "There's too much here. Too many coincidences." Peacock looked up at the ceiling. "You there Clem?"

As he spoke there was a crash directly behind him. He twirled in his seat. A coffee cup lay shattered on the floor behind his chair.

"I saw it fall," Bill said. "It fell off the shelf." He pointed. Against one wall the crew had built shelves to hold the dishes. The coffee cups were kept on an upper

# A Guide to the Ghosts of Lincoln

shelf. The shelf was at least eight inches wide, and all of the other cups were pushed snug against the wall. The cup that had fallen had come from the rear of the wide shelf.

It was a week later that the ghost was first seen.

It was late at night. There were only three members of the crew sleeping upstairs. The others had moved outside into the tent or into the small bedroom on the first floor. Dean was in a deep and sound sleep. His cot was at the foot of the other two cots. Jack and Bill, however, lay awake talking in quiet whispers.

Although they had worked together for well over a month, the two young men had only started to get to know one another. In the late hours their friendship was opening like a flower as they discovered the many things they had in common. It was to be a friendship that would last many years.

"What's your Dad do?" Bill asked, staring into the darkness toward the ceiling.

Jack was silent, then, "He's dead." It was the first time he had had to answer with those words.

"Sorry," Bill said. "When'd he die?"

Jack was only a little surprised to feel the lump rising in his throat. "Two months ago."

"Oh, I am sorry," Bill said softly. "Man, that's pretty recent. It's tough. I know."

Jack was silent.

Bill went on. "My father is dead, too. He died about four years ago. He came home from the dentist, stretched out on the couch and died." Bill chuckled softly. "Talk about having a fear of the dentist! I haven't been to one since!"

Their conversation opened up, and their kinship grew. They spoke softly into the late and moonless hours of the Nebraska summer night. The talk drifted from politics and art to music and religion, and remotely, back to death.

"Do you believe in an afterlife?" Jack asked.

"Yeah, well, I think there is something later." Bill said. "I don't know if it's a heaven or a hell, or just something that lives on. But I believe there is something."

"Same here," Jack said. They fell silent. After a long moment Jack spoke again, but his voice was changed. It now had a tinge of urgency and fear. "Bill," he said, "do you see anything strange in the room right now?"

Bill had noticed it at the same instant. From the darkness of the room a soft, bluish cloud had appeared. Long and slender, in the vague shape of a body, it hung suspended three feet above the cot where Dean continued to snore.

"Do you mean that. . .light over Dean's bed?" Bill said.

"What do you suppose it is?" Jack asked. It had grown a bit in intensity and now cast a faint glow about the room.

Bill raised his hand into the nearly pitch-black air. "It isn't a light from a window," he said. "I'm waving my arm in the air and I don't see any shadow." The old limestone house was nearly a mile from the nearest yard light. There was no traffic on Highway 34 beneath their window.

They watched the light. It did not change for two or three minutes. Then, as they silently watched, it shrank and grew fainter, until it was no longer visible.

"You still there?" Jack asked.

"I don't believe it," Bill stammered.

In the morning they reported their sighting to the rest of the crew. Peacock, the ghost expert, nodded and said, "Man, oh man."

Some nights later a Ouija board was brought out. A few of the crew members huddled together in the darkened main room, their chairs in a tight circle.

Scott left immediately. He wanted to have nothing to do with an attempt at a seance. He retired to his tent and his Bible.

Even the knowledgeable Peacock said that it was bad medicine to fool around with the unknown. Although he watched, he would have nothing to do with the session.

Not much happened with the Ouija board. Questions were asked about the spirit's past, its name and so forth, but nothing concrete could be determined from the responses. As often is with a Ouija board, much more of the energy was spent trying to determine if someone was "cheating" and making the indicator move in a particular direction.

# A Guide to the Ghosts of Lincoln

One thing, however, was certain; on no other night of the summer had the sense of the presence of an unseen spirit been as strong. What had started as an activity for fun and amusement ended with bickering and frayed nerves. And everyone felt it in the air.

Everyone turned in shortly after the board was put away. It was a restless night. Sometime in the darkest hour Jack was awakened by the sounds of people shouting. He lay there an instant and then sprang from his bed and threw on his clothes. He was downstairs before he was even fully awake.

"The hose to the hot water heater has come undone!" the Boss shouted at him. "The basement is flooding. We've got to get the artifacts out of there." He handed Jack a flashlight. "Get to that windmill and shut off the water pump before the entire house is flooded."

He took the flashlight and ran for the back door. He could hear Peacock in the basement struggling with the boxes of artifacts. Jack clicked on the flashlight before he was out of the house. Its strong beam shown through the screen door and into the back yard. It was a good two hundred yards to the water pump across a dark cornfield. He was glad for the light.

As he flew through the back door the flashlight suddenly went dark. He ran past Scott's tent, flicking the switch and pounding the flashlight against his leg in an attempt to get it to work. Still it would not light. He stumbled through the cornfield, trying to pick his way across the rows in the darkness. His shoes were untied and several times he tripped over clods of dirt and fell into the tall corn. The flashlight remained dark.

Finally he stood by the windmill and water pump. From the house he could hear faint calls and shouts. By now the water was spreading over the entire dirt floor of the basement. He smashed the flashlight against his palm, hoping that the shock would give him a small slash of light to find the switch. Nothing. He felt along the old metal until he finally located the switch. He pulled it and heard the soft whir of the pump fall silent.

He hurried back through the cornfield, ignoring the dead flashlight. As he neared the house, Scott appeared from his tent.

"What's going on?" Scott asked.

"A water hose broke," Jack explained. "It flooded the basement."

"I know that," Scott said. "*What's going on?*"

Jack stepped to the screen door and opened it. The instant he stepped back inside the house, the flashlight, now tucked under his arm and forgotten, came on clear and bright.

Another member of the crew came up to him. A wet cigarette dangled from his lips. "It took you long enough," he said. "The entire basement has a foot of water in it.

Jack stared at the flashlight that glared from his cold hand.

The crew member went on. "The hose didn't break," he said vaguely, not removing the cigarette, "it was

# A Guide to the Ghosts of Lincoln

unscrewed from the water heater. Somehow it was *unscrewed from the heater.*"

After that night the crew no longer joked about the spirit. They seldom spoke of it, and never addressed it by their nickname Clem. Occasionally, as the lights would flicker in the evenings, someone would tap out "shave-and-a-haircut" onto the table, and the flickering light would answer "shampoo!" The footsteps during the night continued, and now were located nearly always on the steps that led to the second floor, but little discussion was held among the crew about them. They acknowledged the existence of such apparitions, but did not lend them credence by lengthy discussions.

Peacock now would only enter the house for meals and would leave for his tent immediately after he was finished. Scott refused to enter the house even for his meals.

The job and the summer wound down. Rain delayed the final departure date. Then it cleared and the Boss announced that it would be their last week in the field. It was time to get back to the museum and start to catalogue their work.

It was the second-to-last night they were to spend in the old limestone house. Already most of the crew had started to pack their belongings, anxious to return to the city.

The sun had just set and the sky was still light with dusk. Jack and Peacock stood on the ground just outside the house. Bill was above them, sitting in the windowframe of the second floor. He sat in the darkened window, twirling a flashlight in his hands.

The three of them talked; the conversation was idle, relaxed.

"I'll bet that ole Bill is raring to get back to town and his sweetheart," Peacock laughed.

"Sweetheart?" Jack teased. "Are you kidding? Why, the poor boy doesn't even know what we're talking about. . . ."

They looked up to the window. Bill's head was turned away from them and back into the dark room. He held his hand out, motioning to them. In a moment he looked back down at them. "Ah. . .there's somebody standing here in the room."

Peacock started to say something, but Bill went on.

"There is definitely somebody standing here," Bill said. His voice was urgent, fearful, but strained to keep calm. "There is a man standing in the doorway between the two rooms." He glanced back down to the ground. "There's a kind of a blue glow around him." He turned back into the room, then back down to the two men below him on the ground. "He's still there."

Peacock shouted, "Shine the light on him!"

They could see the flashlight in Bill's hand flick on and light up the room with an eerie yellow glow.

Bill turned off the light. "He's still there. The light went right through him. I turned it off, but he's still there." His voice was shaky, but he continued to report what he saw to them.

# A Guide to the Ghosts of Lincoln

"Wait," Bill said. "He's moving. He's coming. . .no, he's moving backwards, back into the other room. He's gone into the other room. He's gone. I can't see him any more."

Jack and Peacock raced around the corner of the house and flew up the stairs. Bill met them on the tiny staircase, making his way out. Now his voice began to break. "Who was he? I saw him! He. . . !"

The entire event had lasted no more than a minute, but for Bill it would leave its mark for the rest of his life. He had seen something for which there was no explanation in the world of reality most of us would accept as the only world.

Two days later a truck pulled up to the house and the crew loaded supplies and their gear. The two refrigerators were reloaded, and the boxes of artifacts. In a few hours the house stood empty again, and a brown square of dead grass was all that remained where Scott's tent had stood.

Finally, it was time to leave. Everyone but Scott stood near the house a moment or two staring up at it, as a kind of farewell. Scott, however, sat alone in the cab of the big truck, his back to the house and his Bible spread open on his lap.